mastering the pixel 9 and pixel 9 pro

The Ultimate Guide for Beginners and Beyond

scott la counte

RIDICULOUSLY
SIMPLE BOOKS
ANAHEIM, CALIFORNIA

Copyright © 2024 by Scott La Counte

All rights reserved.

No part of this book may be reproduced in any form or by any electronic or mechanical means, including information storage and retrieval systems, without written permission from the author, except for the use of brief quotations in a book review.

contents

Introduction	9
1. MAKING THE SWITCH	13
Why the Pixel 9?	13
Getting Started: Setting Up Your Pixel 9	14
Exploring the Pixel 9's Features	14
Making the Switch: Tips for a Smooth Transition	15
AI on the Phone	16
Pixel Vs…	20
Pixel 9 Pro vs. Pixel 9	20
Pixel 9 Pro vs Pixel 8 Pro	23
Pixel 9 vs Pixel 8	25
Pixel 9 Pro vs Pixel Pro Fold	27
Pixel 9 Pro vs Samsung S24	28
Pixel 9 Pro vs iphone 15 Pro	31
2. GETTING STARTED	35
Setup	35
Finding Your Way Around	55
Feeling Home-less?	70
Get around on your Pixel phone	72
3. THE RIDICULOUSLY SIMPLE OVERVIEW OF ALL THE THINGS YOU SHOULD KNOW	79
Making Pretty Screens	79
A Word, or Two, About Menus	92
Spit Screens	92
Gestures	98
4. THE BASICS…AND KEEP IT RIDICULOUSLY SIMPLE	99
Making Calls	101
Direct My Call	116
Hold For Me	116
Don't Be Spammy	117
Messages	117
Where's An App for That?	123
Driving Directions	127
What's the Name of That Song?	136

Live Captioning	137
Refresh Rate	140
Sharing Wi-Fi	141
Screenshot	143
Google Recorder	147
5. LET'S GO SURFING NOW!	149
Add an Email Account	149
Create and Send an Email	150
Manage Multiple Email Accounts	150
Surfing the Internet	151
6. SNAP IT!	157
The Basics	157
Hello (Photo) Friend	163
Camera Modes	164
Editing Photo	175
Organizing Your Photos	196
Settings	217
7. GOING BEYOND	221
Network & Internet	222
Connected devices	224
Apps	226
Notifications	228
Battery	230
Storage	232
Sound & Vibration	234
Display	236
Wallpaper & Style	238
Accessibility	239
Privacy	241
Security	245
Location	247
Safety & Emergency	249
Car Crash Detection	251
Digital Wellbeing	253
Google	253
System	254
About Phone	255
Tips & support	255
8. CONCLUSION	257

Copyright © 2024 by Scott La Counte.

All rights reserved. No part of this publication may be reproduced, distributed or transmitted in any form or by any means, including photocopying, recording, or other electronic or mechanical methods, without the prior written permission of the publisher, except in the case of brief quotations embodied in critical reviews and certain other noncommercial uses permitted by copyright law.

Limited Liability / Disclaimer of Warranty. While best efforts have been used in preparing this book, the author and publishers make no representations or warranties of any kind and assume no liabilities of any kind with respect to accuracy or completeness of the content and specifically the author nor publisher shall be held liable or responsible to any person or entity with respect to any loss or incidental r consequential damages caused or alleged to have been caused, directly, or indirectly without limitations, by the information or programs contained herein. Furthermore, readers should be aware that the Internet sites listed in this work may have changed or disappeared. This work is sold with the understanding that the advice inside may not be suitable in every situation.

Trademarks. Where trademarks are used in this book this infers no endorsement or any affiliation with this book. Any trademarks (including, but not limiting to, screenshots) used in this book are solely used for editorial and educational purposes.

Disclaimer*: Please note, while every effort has been made to ensure accuracy, this book is not endorsed by Alphabet, Inc. and should be considered unofficial.*

introduction

The Google Pixel series has always been known for pushing the boundaries of smartphone technology, especially when it comes to photography and software. Ever since the first Pixel hit the shelves, it's stood out from the crowd, blending Google's AI with hardware that just works. With each new model, the Pixel series has gotten even better, setting the standard for what an Android phone can be. The Pixel 9 is no different.

a refined design for a new era

At first glance, the Pixel 9 showcases a design that builds on the aesthetic foundations laid by its predecessors. The iconic camera visor, a signature feature since the Pixel 6, remains a prominent element but with a more sophisticated, pill-shaped design. This new iteration of the visor is sleeker and integrates more naturally with the phone's overall design.

The build quality of the Pixel 9 is another area where Google has made noticeable improvements. The phone's glass front and back, both protected by Corning Gorilla Glass Victus 2, are complemented by an aluminum frame that adds durability without compromising on aesthetics. This premium construction not only feels great in the hand but also offers peace of mind, knowing that the phone can withstand the occasional drop or scratch. The Pixel 9 is also IP68 rated, meaning it is resistant to dust and can survive

Introduction

submersion in water up to 1.5 meters for 30 minutes. This level of durability makes the Pixel 9 as rugged as it is stylish.

One of the most appreciated design choices is the flat display panel. Unlike some other smartphones that feature curved or "waterfall" displays, the Pixel 9's flat screen is easier to handle, reducing accidental touches and making it more comfortable to hold. This squared-off design not only improves grip but also contributes to the phone's overall usability. However, it's worth noting that the glossy edges of the Pro models tend to attract fingerprints, which means you might find yourself wiping them down more often than you'd like.

display brilliance

The Pixel 9 series continues Google's tradition of delivering outstanding displays. The standard Pixel 9 comes equipped with a 6.3-inch OLED display, which, while slightly larger than the Pixel 8's 6.2-inch screen, offers a significant upgrade in terms of brightness and clarity. With a resolution of 1080 x 2424 pixels and a peak brightness of 2700 nits, the Pixel 9's display is not only sharp and vibrant but also exceptionally bright. This makes it one of the best displays on the market, perfect for viewing content in any lighting condition, including direct sunlight.

The always-on display feature returns, providing at-a-glance information such as the time, date, and notifications without needing to unlock the phone. This is a staple of the Pixel series that users have come to appreciate for its convenience and efficiency.

performance powerhouse

Under the hood, the Pixel 9 is powered by Google's latest Tensor G4 chipset. This 4nm octa-core processor represents a significant leap forward from the Tensor G3 used in the Pixel 8. The G4's improved architecture ensures faster processing speeds and greater efficiency, making the Pixel 9 not only more powerful but also better at conserving battery life. Paired with 12GB of RAM, the Pixel 9 is more than capable of handling multitasking, gaming, and other demanding tasks with ease.

Why does this processing power matter? A little later, I'll talk about AI on the phone, and that's where this power is really needed. Yes, there's other tasks that the G4 excels at, but AI is the standout feature of this phone.

camera capabilities

The main camera consists of a 50 MP wide lens and a 48 MP ultrawide lens. This combination allows users to capture everything from expansive landscapes to detailed close-ups with stunning clarity. The inclusion of features like single-zone laser autofocus, Pixel Shift, and Ultra-HDR ensures that photos are sharp, well-exposed, and rich in color.

The selfie camera on the Pixel 9 is a 10.5 MP sensor that offers excellent performance, particularly in well-lit conditions. It supports 4K video recording, making it ideal for video calls and social media content creation. The Pixel 9's camera system is designed to excel in a variety of shooting conditions, whether you're capturing a sunset or a dimly lit room.

One of the standout features of the Pixel 9's camera is its AI-driven image processing. Google has refined its algorithms to deliver even better results than before, particularly in low-light scenarios. The Pixel 9's Night Sight mode, for example, allows users to take clear, detailed photos in near-darkness without the need for a flash.

battery life and charging

Battery life is a critical aspect of any smartphone, and the Pixel 9 is equipped with a 4700 mAh battery that provides solid endurance. Thanks to the efficiency of the Tensor G4 chipset, the Pixel 9 can easily last a full day of moderate to heavy use.

When it's time to recharge, the Pixel 9 supports 27W wired charging, which can bring the battery up to 55% in just 30 minutes. The phone also supports 15W wireless charging with the Pixel Stand, as well as reverse wireless charging, which allows you to charge other devices like earbuds or a smartwatch directly from your phone.

Introduction

what's new and notable

The Pixel 9 series introduces several new features that set it apart from previous models. One of the most notable is the inclusion of Satellite SOS service, which allows users to send emergency messages even when they're outside of cellular coverage. This feature is particularly valuable for outdoor enthusiasts or anyone who spends time in remote areas where traditional networks may not be available.

Another significant improvement is the ultrasonic fingerprint sensor, which is more reliable and faster than the optical sensors used in previous models. This upgrade brings the Pixel 9 in line with other flagship smartphones, offering a more secure and responsive biometric option.

Additionally, the Pixel 9 introduces enhanced AI features, including more advanced voice commands, better image processing, and improved real-time translations.

1 /
making the switch

SO THE PIXEL SOUNDS SWELL, right? Good enough to buy this book. But what if you've never used a Pixel? Or what if you've never used an iPhone? Android is completely new to you.

Transitioning to the Pixel 9 is smoother than you might think, and with a little guidance, you'll soon feel right at home with your new device.

why the pixel 9?

Let's start with why the Pixel 9 is an excellent choice, regardless of your origin. Google's Pixel phones have always been designed with a focus on simplicity, usability, and the best of what Android offers.

For Android users, the Pixel 9 offers the purest Android experience available. This means you get to enjoy Android 14 as Google intended it, free from the bloatware and unnecessary customizations that often come with other Android devices. The interface is clean, the updates are prompt, and the integration with Google's services is seamless. If you're coming from another Android device, you'll appreciate the familiarity of the operating system, but you'll also notice how much smoother and more polished everything feels on the Pixel 9.

If you're switching from an iPhone, the Pixel 9 offers a fresh perspective. Google has worked hard to make Android competitive with iOS and, in many ways, even more customizable and flexible. While the switch might seem like a big change, especially if you've been in the Apple ecosystem for years, the Pixel 9's design and features are intuitive enough that you'll quickly get the hang of things.

getting started: setting up your pixel 9

The first step in making the switch is setting up your new Pixel 9. Google has made this process as simple as possible, whether you're coming from another Android device or an iPhone.

If you're switching from an Android device, the process is straightforward. When you power on your Pixel 9 for the first time, you'll be guided through the setup process. Google provides an option to transfer your data from your old phone, including your apps, contacts, photos, and even your home screen layout. You only need your old device, a cable to connect the two phones, and a few minutes of patience. Google's data transfer tool is fast and efficient, ensuring you don't lose any critical information in the switch.

The process is just as simple for iPhone users, although it may require a bit more time, depending on how much data you have to transfer. Google has a dedicated tool called "Switch to Android," which you can download from the App Store on your iPhone. This app will guide you through transferring your contacts, messages, photos, and more to your new Pixel 9. The tool even helps you transfer your iCloud data, making sure that your photos and contacts come with you to your new device.

Once the data transfer is complete, the Pixel 9 will be set up and ready to go with all your essentials in place. Your apps will download automatically, and your contacts and messages will be waiting for you.

exploring the pixel 9's features

The Pixel 9 isn't just about a clean interface—it's packed with features that make it a powerful tool for everyday life. Here are a few highlights that you'll want to explore as you get to know your new phone.

1. Google Assistant and AI Integration: The Pixel 9 takes full advantage of Google's AI capabilities, making it one of the smartest smartphones available. Google Assistant is built into the phone and can be summoned with a simple "Hey Google" or by squeezing the sides of the device. Whether you

need help setting reminders, sending texts, or finding the nearest coffee shop, Google Assistant is there to make your life easier. And with the Pixel 9's AI-driven features like Call Screen, which helps you avoid spam calls, and Now Playing, which identifies songs playing in your environment, you'll find that your phone is constantly working to make your day smoother.

2. Camera Capabilities: One of the standout features of the Pixel series has always been its camera, and the Pixel 9 is no exception. Google's AI-enhanced camera system is designed to make taking great photos easy, even if you're not a photography expert. Features like Night Sight for low-light photography, Super Res Zoom for clear zoomed-in shots, and Magic Eraser for removing unwanted objects from your photos are all powered by AI, ensuring that your pictures come out looking professional every time. If you're switching from an iPhone, you'll find that the Pixel 9's camera can easily hold its own, offering some of the best smartphone photography available today.

3. Seamless Integration with Google Services: If you're already using Google services like Gmail, Google Calendar, or Google Photos, you'll find that the Pixel 9 integrates seamlessly with these apps. Your emails, appointments, and photos are automatically synced with your phone, making it easy to stay organized and on top of things. And with 7 years of guaranteed updates, your Pixel 9 will stay current with the latest software features and security patches, ensuring that your phone remains a reliable companion for years to come.

making the switch: tips for a smooth transition

Switching to a new phone, especially one with a different operating system, can feel like a big change, but with the right approach, it doesn't have to be overwhelming. Here are a few tips to help make your transition to the Pixel 9 as smooth as possible:

1. Take Your Time: Don't feel like you have to learn everything about your new phone simultaneously. Spend some time exploring the Pixel 9 at your own pace. Google provides plenty of tips and tutorials within the settings menu, and the Pixel Tips app offers helpful advice on how to get the most out of your new device.

2. Customize Your Experience: One of Android's strengths is its

customization options. Spend time personalizing your home screen, experimenting with different widgets, and exploring the various themes and wallpapers available. The more your phone reflects your style, the more comfortable you'll feel using it.

3. Explore the Play Store: The Google Play Store is home to millions of apps, including many you may have used on your previous device. Take some time to browse the store and download the apps you need. You'll likely find that many of your favorite apps are available on Android, and you might even discover some new ones that enhance your experience.

4. Don't Be Afraid to Ask for Help: If you're unsure about something, Google's support resources can help. The Pixel 9 includes a built-in support app that connects you with Google's customer service, and the online Pixel community is a great place to ask questions and share tips with other users.

ai on the phone

When it comes to Pixel, one thing you'll hear a lot is the word "AI"; unless you've been living under a rock for the past few years, then I'm sure you've heard about AI. Even still, people have a lot of misconceptions about it. So let's start with an introduction about what AI is (and isn't), then look at how it works on the Pixel.

What Is AI

Artificial Intelligence (AI) refers to the capacity of devices such as computers, robots, and phones to execute tasks that typically require human intellect. These activities vary from simple functions like recognizing, objects in an image to sophisticated processes like solving problems, making decisions, and acquiring knowledge through experience.

Reflecting on how humans gain knowledge and make decisions can help us understand AI. When we master riding a bicycle, our brain processes aspects such as balance, speed, direction, and feedback from previous tries. Similarly, AI functions by absorbing information, gradually enhancing its abilities without manual reprogramming. There are diverse types of AI aiming to imitate features of human intelligence. The basic form known as AI is designed for tasks like responding to users, answering questions through virtual assistants, or managing email.

On the other hand, AI introduces the idea of performing duties like a human being, albeit its practical implementation remains largely theoretical. AI systems are developed based on algorithms, rules, or instructions that direct machines to solve problems. These algorithms are provided with large data sets, enabling the AI to undergo training and improve its accuracy.

Machine learning, a subset of AI, plays a crucial role in enhancing the functions of these systems. Rather than being programmed directly, machine learning AI processes data using statistical methods to unveil patterns within the information. Deep learning represents a specialized form of machine learning that employs neural networks inspired by the functions of the human brain. This methodology analyzes extensive data sets through layers, allowing the AI to understand and interpret complex patterns.

AI is integrated into aspects of society, from personalized content recommendations on streaming platforms to roles in industries like healthcare finance and autonomous vehicles. It offers potential benefits such as breaking language barriers and aiding research efforts. In the realm of smartphones, AI enhances the user experience in ways including elevating camera quality and providing virtual assistants.

Exploring AI provides a peek into the upcoming technological landscape, where machines adapt and interact with the world, moving us closer to unleashing human capacity for innovation.

AI On the Pixel

Now that you have a pretty broad overview of what AI is, let's see how Google has taken advantage of it on the Pixel

AI is no longer just a feature on the Pixel—the beating heart drives the entire experience, making the Pixel 9 a truly smart smartphone. From enhancing photos to providing real-time assistance, the Pixel 9 uses AI to anticipate your needs and make everyday tasks more accessible, intuitive, and enjoyable.

At the core of the Pixel 9's AI capabilities is Google's Tensor G4 chipset. This powerful processor is designed to handle the most demanding AI tasks directly on the device, reducing the need to rely on cloud-based processing. It's like having a supercomputer in your pocket, always learning and adapting to your preferences and habits.

One of the most noticeable ways AI comes to life on the Pixel 9 is through the new and improved Google Assistant, powered by the Gemini AI system. Gemini is faster and more capable than previous versions of Google's assistant, offering more natural and context-aware interactions. Whether you're asking it to set reminders, control smart home devices, or find information online, Gemini responds quickly and accurately, understanding the nuances of your requests better than ever before.

A cool feature is the "Ask About This Screen" functionality, where Gemini can analyze the content currently displayed on your phone and provide relevant information or actions. For example, if you're watching a YouTube video about restaurants in a new city, Gemini can pull up a list of those restaurants in Google Maps with a simple command. This contextual awareness means you spend less time navigating apps and more time getting the information you need.

Taking inspiration from AI-driven chatbots like ChatGPT, Google has introduced Gemini Live, a feature that allows for real-time voice conversations with your phone. This isn't just another voice command feature—Gemini Live can engage in natural, flowing conversations, allowing you to pause, interrupt, or pick up a conversation later, even if your screen is locked. It's like conversing with a knowledgeable friend who's always available to help, whether you're exploring deep questions about the universe or simply asking for the weather forecast.

For users who own the new Pixel Buds Pro 2, Gemini Live becomes even more versatile. You can engage in conversations with Gemini directly through your earbuds, making it easier to access AI-driven assistance on the go without needing to pull out your phone.

Photography has always been a strong suit for the Pixel series, and the Pixel 9 pushes the boundaries of what's possible with smartphone cameras, thanks to AI. The new Magic Editor feature allows users to "reimagine" their photos in ways that were previously only possible with advanced photo editing software. With just a few taps and text prompts, you can completely transform a scene—change the sky from cloudy to sunny, add objects that weren't there before, or enhance certain aspects of the image to make it look more professional.

This level of control and creativity is unprecedented on a smartphone. Whether you're a casual photographer or a social media influencer, the Pixel 9's AI-driven editing tools give you the power to create stunning images that reflect your vision, no matter the conditions when you take the shot.

Another innovative feature is "Add Me," which solves the age-old problem of group photos where someone always has to be behind the camera. With Add Me, you can take a picture of your friends, then step into the frame yourself, and the Pixel 9 will seamlessly stitch the images together. The result is a group photo where everyone is included, without asking a stranger for help. This feature uses augmented reality (AR) overlays to ensure perfect framing, making it easy to create natural-looking group photos every time.

In addition to enhancing photography, Google has introduced AI features that make managing phone calls easier and more efficient. One such feature is Call Notes, which uses AI to summarize your phone conversations after you hang up. Imagine you're calling around for quotes on car repairs or trying to remember the details of a doctor's appointment—Call Notes automatically transcribes the key points, so you don't have to worry about taking notes yourself.

This feature is handy when you forget to jot down important information during a call. The best part? All this processing happens on the device, so your conversations remain private and secure, never being sent to the cloud. Call Notes also ensures everyone on the call knows it's being transcribed, maintaining transparency and trust.

Google has also introduced several new apps and features that leverage AI to simplify everyday tasks. Pixel Screenshots, for example, uses AI to understand the context of your screenshots, making it easier to find and organize them. Whether it's a recipe, an address, or an event you've saved, Pixel Screenshots lets you search through your images using conversational queries, saving you time and hassle.

Pixel Studio is another exciting addition, allowing users to create illustrations and custom stickers from their photos using text prompts. This creative tool is perfect for personalizing your messages or creating unique digital art, and it's powered by a combination of on-device AI and Google's Imagen 3 cloud-based model. The ability to generate art and illustrations directly on your phone opens up new possibilities for creativity right at your fingertips.

The Pixel 9 series is not just about what AI can do today but also about what it promises for the future. Google has laid the groundwork for even more advanced AI features that will continue to roll out over time. From more profound integration with personal assistants to more sophisticated AI-driven photography and editing tools, the Pixel 9 is designed to evolve, ensuring it remains at the cutting edge of smartphone technology.

As AI advances, the Pixel 9 series stands ready to harness these developments, making it not just a smartphone but a personal assistant, a creative studio, and a powerful tool for navigating the complexities of modern life.

pixel vs...

Before moving on to how the phone works, let's compare it to other smartphones. This section will help if you are still on the fence about buying a Pixel and if you are confused about how your phone differs from something someone else has. If you aren't interested, just skip this section.

pixel 9 pro vs. pixel 9

To start things off, let's look at what's the big difference between the base Pixel 9 and the one that has the fancy "Pro" attached to it.

At first glance, both the Pixel 9 and Pixel 9 Pro share a striking resemblance, not just in design but also in their overall dimensions. Each device measures 152.8 x 72 x 8.5 mm, a deliberate choice by Google to ensure that the phones are easy to handle and carry, fitting comfortably in the user's hand or pocket. This design consistency extends to the build quality, with both models featuring a glass front and back, protected by Corning Gorilla Glass Victus 2, and an aluminum frame that lends a premium feel to the devices. Despite the similarities in their physical characteristics, the Pixel 9 is marginally lighter at 198 grams compared to the 199 grams of the Pixel 9 Pro, a difference so slight that it's nearly invisible in everyday use.

Where the Pixel 9 and Pixel 9 Pro begin to diverge is in their displays. The Pixel 9 Pro is equipped with a 6.3-inch LTPO OLED display that supports a peak brightness of 3000 nits, setting a new benchmark for screen visibility,

Mastering the Pixel 9 and Pixel 9 Pro

even under direct sunlight. This display also boasts a resolution of 1280 x 2856 pixels, delivering a pixel density of approximately 495 ppi, which ensures sharp and vibrant visuals.

In contrast, the Pixel 9 features a 6.3-inch OLED display, slightly less advanced than the LTPO panel of the Pro model. The Pixel 9's screen peaks at 2700 nits, still highly impressive, and offers a resolution of 1080 x 2424 pixels, resulting in a pixel density of about 422 ppi. While this display is slightly less sharp and bright than that of the Pixel 9 Pro, it still delivers an excellent viewing experience.

Underneath the hood, both models are powered by Google's latest Tensor G4 chipset. This chipset includes an octa-core CPU, with a high-performance Cortex-X4 core clocked at 3.1 GHz, three Cortex-A720 cores running at 2.6 GHz, and four Cortex-A520 cores at 1.92 GHz. This configuration ensures that both the Pixel 9 and Pixel 9 Pro easily handle multitasking, gaming, and other demanding applications.

However, when it comes to memory, the Pixel 9 Pro takes a clear lead. The Pro model offers up to 16GB of RAM across all its storage variants, which include 128GB, 256GB, 512GB, and even a 1TB option. This abundance of RAM ensures that the Pixel 9 Pro can handle more apps running simultaneously and switch between tasks with minimal lag. The Pixel 9, while still powerful, is slightly more modest in this department, offering 12GB of RAM and storage options limited to 128GB and 256GB. For most users, this configuration will be more than sufficient, but power users may appreciate the extra headroom provided by the Pixel 9 Pro.

Camera technology has long been a defining feature of the Pixel series, and the 2024 models continue this tradition with upgrades. The Pixel 9 Pro sports a triple-camera system, including a 50 MP wide lens, a 48 MP periscope telephoto lens, and a 48 MP ultrawide lens. This setup is designed to cover a wide range of photographic scenarios, from capturing expansive landscapes to zooming in on distant subjects with clarity and detail. Including features like multi-zone laser autofocus, Pixel Shift, and Ultra-HDR further enhances the photographic capabilities of the Pixel 9 Pro, making it a versatile tool for both amateur and professional photographers.

While slightly less equipped, the Pixel 9 still offers a formidable camera setup. It features a dual-camera system with a 50 MP wide lens and a 48 MP ultrawide lens. While it lacks the periscope telephoto lens found in the Pro model, the Pixel 9 still delivers excellent photo quality, especially with the help of Google's computational photography algorithms. Including single-zone laser autofocus and Ultra-HDR ensures that users can capture detailed and vibrant images in various lighting conditions.

Both models excel in video recording, though the Pixel 9 Pro once again has the edge with its ability to record in 8K at 30fps. This capability lets users capture video with incredible detail, making the Pixel 9 Pro an attractive option for those who prioritize video quality. The Pixel 9, while limited to 4K recording at 60fps, still offers excellent video performance and is suitable for most users' needs.

Selfie enthusiasts will appreciate the upgrades in the Pixel 9 Pro, which features a 42 MP ultrawide front-facing camera. This significant increase in resolution compared to the Pixel 9's 10.5 MP front camera means the Pixel 9 Pro delivers sharper and more detailed selfies, making it ideal for users who frequently capture front-facing photos or videos.

Battery life is another area where these models exhibit differences that may influence a user's choice. The Pixel 9 and Pixel 9 Pro are equipped with a 4700 mAh battery, sufficient for a full day of use under normal conditions. However, the Pixel 9 Pro supports faster wireless charging speeds of up to 21W with the Pixel Stand, compared to 15W for the Pixel 9.

Connectivity options remain robust across both models, supporting the latest wireless standards, including Wi-Fi 7, Bluetooth 5.3, and NFC. The Pixel 9 Pro introduces Ultra Wideband (UWB) support, which enhances location tracking and enables more precise device interactions. This addition, along with the Satellite SOS service, makes the Pixel 9 Pro a more attractive option for users who value cutting-edge connectivity features.

In terms of software, both the Pixel 9 and Pixel 9 Pro run on Android 14. Google promises up to seven major Android upgrades, ensuring that these devices remain up-to-date with the latest features and security patches for years to come.

The Pixel 9 Pro is ideal for users who demand the very best in display technology, camera performance, and connectivity features. At the same time, the Pixel 9 offers a more balanced approach, delivering high-end features at a more accessible price point.

pixel 9 pro vs pixel 8 pro

So now you know how the current models compare, but how about last years models? Let's start by comparing the 9 Pro to the 8 Pro from last year.

Starting with the design, the Pixel 9 Pro has undergone a subtle but significant transformation compared to the Pixel 8 Pro. The new model is slightly smaller and lighter, with dimensions of 152.8 x 72 x 8.5 mm and a weight of 199 grams, compared to the Pixel 8 Pro's 162.6 x 76.5 x 8.8 mm and 213 grams. These changes make the Pixel 9 Pro more ergonomic and easier to handle, appealing to users who prioritize a comfortable grip and pocketability. Both devices are constructed with premium materials, featuring a glass front and back protected by Gorilla Glass Victus 2 and an aluminum frame, ensuring durability and a sleek aesthetic. The IP68 dust and water resistance rating remains unchanged, allowing both phones to survive in up to 1.5 meters of water for 30 minutes.

One of the most noticeable differences between the two models lies in their displays. The Pixel 8 Pro boasts a larger 6.7-inch LTPO OLED display with a resolution of 1344 x 2992 pixels, offering a pixel density of approximately 489 ppi. This display, capable of reaching a peak brightness of 2400 nits, is vivid and sharp, providing an excellent viewing experience. The Pixel 9 Pro, however, features a slightly smaller 6.3-inch LTPO OLED display with a resolution of 1280 x 2856 pixels and a higher pixel density of around 495 ppi. What the Pixel 9 Pro loses in screen size, it gains in brightness, with a peak output of 3000 nits, making it one of the brightest displays on the market. This increase in brightness ensures that the Pixel 9 Pro remains highly visible even in direct sunlight.

Under the hood, the Pixel 9 Pro sees a substantial upgrade with the introduction of the Google Tensor G4 chipset. This 4nm octa-core processor includes a 3.1 GHz Cortex-X4 core, three Cortex-A720 cores at 2.6 GHz, and four Cortex-A520 cores at 1.92 GHz. This setup delivers faster and more efficient performance than the Pixel 8 Pro's Tensor G3 chipset, which features a nona-core configuration with a 3.0 GHz Cortex-X3 core, four Cortex-A715 cores at 2.45 GHz, and four Cortex-A510 cores at 2.15 GHz. The new Tensor G4 not only improves overall speed but also enhances energy efficiency, allowing the Pixel 9 Pro to handle demanding tasks more effectively while conserving battery life.

The GPU also sees an upgrade, with the Pixel 9 Pro featuring the Mali-G715 MC7, compared to the Immortalis-G715s MC10 found in the Pixel 8 Pro. This new GPU offers better graphics performance, particularly in gaming and video rendering, ensuring a smoother and more immersive experience for users who enjoy graphically intensive applications.

Memory and storage options have also been improved in the Pixel 9 Pro. While both models offer UFS 3.1 storage technology, the Pixel 9 Pro comes with 16GB of RAM across all its storage variants, which include 128GB, 256GB, 512GB, and 1TB options. In contrast, the Pixel 8 Pro offers 12GB of RAM with the same storage options. The increase in RAM allows the Pixel 9 Pro to handle more apps and processes simultaneously without compromising performance, making it a better choice for power users who require multitasking capabilities.

The Pixel 9 Pro features a triple-camera setup on the rear, consisting of a 50 MP wide lens, a 48 MP periscope telephoto lens with 5x optical zoom, and a 48 MP ultrawide lens. This setup is similar to the Pixel 8 Pro, which also includes a 50 MP wide lens, a 48 MP periscope telephoto lens with 5x optical zoom, and a 48 MP ultrawide lens. However, the Pixel 9 Pro introduces enhancements like Multi-zone Laser AF, Pixel Shift, Ultra-HDR, and Zoom Enhance, which elevate the overall photography experience by providing sharper images, better low-light performance, and improved zoom capabilities.

The front-facing camera on the Pixel 9 Pro is another area where Google has made significant strides. The new model features a 42 MP ultrawide camera, a substantial upgrade from the Pixel 8 Pro's 10.5 MP front camera.

Battery life is always a critical factor for smartphone users, and while both models are designed to last a full day under normal use, the Pixel 9 Pro offers a slightly smaller 4700 mAh battery compared to the 5050 mAh battery in the Pixel 8 Pro. Despite the smaller battery, the Pixel 9 Pro benefits from the more efficient Tensor G4 chipset and software optimizations in Android 14, which help to maintain battery life on par with or better than the Pixel 8 Pro. The Pixel 9 Pro also supports 27W wired charging and 21W wireless charging with the Pixel Stand, allowing users to quickly recharge their devices. The Pixel 8 Pro, by comparison, supports 30W wired charging and 23W wireless charging, which are slightly faster but do not make a significant difference in everyday use.

In terms of software, both the Pixel 9 Pro and Pixel 8 Pro run on Android 14, with Google promising up to seven major Android upgrades for each device.

The Pixel 9 Pro represents a thoughtful evolution over the Pixel 8 Pro, with improvements in display brightness, camera technology, processing power, and overall user experience. While the Pixel 8 Pro remains a strong contender in the smartphone market, the Pixel 9 Pro's enhancements make it a compelling upgrade for those who demand the best in mobile technology.

pixel 9 vs pixel 8

Now let's turn things around and look at the base Pixel 9 as it compares to last years Pixel 8.

Measuring 152.8 x 72 x 8.5 mm and weighing 198 grams, the Pixel 9 is slightly larger and heavier than the Pixel 8, which had dimensions of 150.5 x 70.8 x 8.9 mm and weighed 187 grams. This increase in size and weight is subtle but noticeable, offering a more substantial feel in the hand without compromising on comfort or ergonomics. The Pixel 9 continues the tradition of using premium materials, with a glass front and back protected by Corning Gorilla Glass Victus 2, and an aluminum frame that ensures durability while maintaining a sleek and modern aesthetic.

In comparison, the Pixel 8 also featured a glass front and back, protected by the first generation of Gorilla Glass Victus, and an aluminum frame. The Pixel 8's slightly smaller size and lighter weight made it more pocket-friendly, but the Pixel 9's refined dimensions and enhanced build quality contribute to a more premium feel overall. Both devices boast an IP68 rating, ensuring they are dustproof and water-resistant up to 1.5 meters for 30 minutes, making them resilient against the elements and everyday accidents.

Display quality has always been a critical aspect of the Pixel series, and both the Pixel 9 and Pixel 8 deliver impressive visual experiences. The Pixel 9 is equipped with a 6.3-inch OLED display, slightly larger than the Pixel 8's 6.2-inch screen. Despite the marginal difference in size, the Pixel 9's display significantly improves brightness and clarity. With a resolution of 1080 x 2424 pixels and a pixel density of approximately 422 ppi, the Pixel 9's screen is sharp and vibrant. It also supports HDR10+ and can reach a peak brightness of 2700 nits, making it one of the brightest displays on the market.

Performance is another area where the Pixel 9 sees significant advancements over its predecessor. The Pixel 9 is powered by Google's latest Tensor G4 chipset, a 4nm octa-core processor that includes a 3.1 GHz Cortex-X4 core, three Cortex-A720 cores at 2.6 GHz, and four Cortex-A520 cores at 1.92 GHz. This configuration delivers improved speed and efficiency compared to the Pixel 8, which is equipped with the Google Tensor G3 chipset, a 4nm nona-core processor that features a 3.0 GHz Cortex-X3 core, four Cortex-A715 cores at 2.45 GHz, and four Cortex-A510 cores at 2.15 GHz.

Google's Pixel phones are renowned for their camera capabilities, and the Pixel 9 continues this legacy with a dual-camera setup that builds on the strengths of the Pixel 8. The Pixel 9 features a 50 MP wide lens paired with a 48 MP ultrawide lens, offering versatility and high-quality imaging across a range of scenarios. The main camera includes advanced features such as single-zone laser autofocus, Pixel Shift, Ultra-HDR, and the Best Take function, all of which contribute to sharper images, better low-light performance, and more dynamic range in photos.

The Pixel 8, while also impressive, features a dual-camera system with a 50 MP wide lens and a 12 MP ultrawide lens. The Pixel 8's camera setup is slightly less powerful in terms of resolution, particularly with the ultrawide lens, which is where the Pixel 9's enhancements are most evident. Both phones offer 4K video recording at multiple frame rates and 10-bit HDR, but the Pixel 9's improved hardware and software algorithms ensure that it delivers superior image and video quality, especially in challenging lighting conditions.

The front-facing camera on the Pixel 9 is a 10.5 MP sensor, similar to the Pixel 8, but with enhanced features that improve its performance. Both devices support 4K video recording on the front camera, making them ideal for video calls and social media content creation.

The Pixel 9 represents a significant upgrade over the Pixel 8, offering improvements in display quality, processing power, camera capabilities, and battery life. While the Pixel 8 remains a strong contender in the mid-range smartphone market, the Pixel 9's enhancements make it a compelling choice for users who demand more from their devices.

pixel 9 pro vs pixel pro fold

While this book focuses on the Pixel 9 and Pixel 9 Pro, there is another Pixel phone generating a lot of good buzz: the Pixel Pro Fold. As the name implies, the Pixel Pro Fold is Google's foldable device. What's great about the phone is that the experience is essentially the same, even on the foldable phone.

The idea of folding a phone in two sounds cool and even futuristic, but it comes at a pretty steep price; let's compare the Pixel 9 Pro to the Pixel Fold Pro and see if the price difference is worth it.

We'll skip over the dimensions because, on a foldable, that's not as important; of course, the phone that folds out will be bigger. Unfolded, it's pretty close to the same size. It's about 50 grams heavier, but again, it's kind of expected, considering it's bigger.

Display technology is one of the most significant areas where these two devices diverge. The Pixel 9 Pro features a 6.3-inch LTPO OLED display with a resolution of 1280 x 2856 pixels, delivering a sharp 495 ppi density. This display supports HDR10+ and boasts an impressive peak brightness of 3000 nits, ensuring vivid colors and clear visibility even in the brightest sunlight. The 120Hz refresh rate ensures smooth scrolling and fluid animations, enhancing the overall user experience.

The Pixel Fold 9 Pro, however, offers a dual-display experience. Its main attraction is the 8.0-inch foldable LTPO OLED screen with a resolution of 2076 x 2152 pixels, providing a more immersive experience with a 373 ppi density. While it has a lower pixel density compared to the Pixel 9 Pro, the Fold 9 Pro's expansive display is designed for multitasking and media consumption, offering more screen real estate for productivity or entertainment. The cover display, used when the device is folded, is a 6.3-inch OLED panel with a resolution of 1080 x 2424 pixels and a density of 422 ppi, which is comparable to the Pixel 9 Pro's display in terms of clarity and brightness. Both displays support HDR10+ and offer peak brightness levels of 2700 nits for the main screen and 1800 nits for the cover screen, making them versatile and capable in various lighting conditions.

Camera technology is another area where the Pixel 9 Pro and Pixel Fold 9 Pro differ significantly despite offering high-quality imaging capabilities. The Pixel 9 Pro has a triple-camera setup on the rear, featuring a 50 MP wide lens, a 48 MP periscope telephoto lens with 5x optical zoom, and a 48 MP ultrawide lens. This array allows users to capture various scenes, from expansive landscapes to detailed close-ups, with features like multi-zone laser autofocus, Ultra-HDR, and Pixel Shift enhancing the photographic experience. The front-facing camera is a powerful 42 MP sensor, making it ideal for high-quality selfies and video calls.

The Pixel Fold 9 Pro while offering a triple-camera system, takes a slightly different approach. Its primary camera is a 48 MP wide lens, a 10.8 MP telephoto lens with 5x optical zoom, and a 10.5 MP ultrawide lens. Although the megapixel count is lower than that of the Pixel 9 Pro, the Fold 9 Pro's camera system is optimized for versatility and usability in both folded and unfolded states. The Fold 9 Pro's selfie cameras, one on the main display and another on the cover display are both 10 MP sensors, providing consistent image quality whether the device is folded or unfolded. While the Pixel 9 Pro excels in raw photographic power, the Fold 9 Pro offers more flexibility in capturing your images, catering to users who value adaptability.

The Pixel 9 Pro and Pixel Fold 9 Pro represent two different approaches to the future of smartphones. The Pixel 9 Pro is ideal for users who seek a traditional, high-performance smartphone with top-tier camera capabilities and a compact, durable design. On the other hand, the Pixel Fold 9 Pro is designed for those who demand versatility and productivity from their devices, offering a unique foldable experience that bridges the gap between a smartphone and a tablet.

pixel 9 pro vs samsung s24

Let's look now at how the Pixel 9 Pro compares to the two most used phones out there. We'll start with the Samsung S24 Ultra. Like Google, Samsung offers several phone choices, but we'll focus on how the best Pixel phone compares to the best Samsung phone.

Starting with the design, both devices exude a premium feel, but they cater to slightly different tastes. The Pixel 9 Pro is more compact, with dimensions of 152.8 x 72 x 8.5 mm and a weight of 199 grams. It features a glass front and back protected by Corning Gorilla Glass Victus 2 and an aluminum frame, giving it a sleek yet sturdy build. The Samsung S24 Ultra is larger and heavier, measuring 162.3 x 79 x 8.6 mm and weighing 232 grams. Its design includes a glass front and back made from Corning Gorilla Armor, coupled with a titanium frame, which adds to its robustness and premium aesthetic. The S24 Ultra also comes with a built-in stylus, an iconic feature of Samsung's Ultra models, which is integrated with Bluetooth and sensors like an accelerometer and gyro, making it a versatile tool for productivity.

When it comes to display technology, both Google and Samsung have pushed the envelope. The Pixel 9 Pro sports a 6.3-inch LTPO OLED display with a resolution of 1280 x 2856 pixels and a peak brightness of 3000 nits.

Samsung's S24 Ultra, however, takes the display game even further. It features a larger 6.8-inch Dynamic LTPO AMOLED 2X display with a resolution of 1440 x 3120 pixels and a peak brightness of 2600 nits. While slightly less bright than the Pixel 9 Pro, the S24 Ultra's display offers a higher resolution and a larger screen area, which is particularly appealing for users who consume a lot of media or enjoy gaming.

Under the hood, both phones are powered by some of the most advanced processors available. The Pixel 9 Pro is equipped with Google's Tensor G4 chipset, a 4nm octa-core processor that includes a 3.1 GHz Cortex-X4 core, three Cortex-A720 cores at 2.6 GHz, and four Cortex-A520 cores at 1.92 GHz. This setup ensures that the Pixel 9 Pro can handle demanding tasks with ease, from gaming to multitasking, all while maintaining energy efficiency.

The Samsung S24 Ultra, on the other hand, is powered by the Qualcomm Snapdragon 8 Gen 3, also built on a 4nm process. This chipset features an 8-core configuration with a higher clock speed, including a 3.39GHz Cortex-X4 core, three Cortex-A720 cores at 3.1 GHz, two Cortex-A720 cores at 2.9 GHz, and two Cortex-A520 cores at 2.2 GHz. The S24 Ultra's processor is complemented by the Adreno 750 GPU, which is clocked at 1 GHz, providing superior graphics performance, particularly in gaming and high-resolution video playback. While both phones offer exceptional performance, the S24 Ultra's slightly more powerful processor gives it an edge in handling the most demanding applications.

Memory and storage are crucial for users who multitask or store large amounts of data on their devices. The Pixel 9 Pro offers 16GB of RAM across all its storage options, which range from 128GB to 1TB, all using UFS 3.1 technology. This ample memory ensures that the device can handle multiple apps running simultaneously without slowing down.

Samsung, while offering slightly less RAM at 12GB across its storage variants, compensates with faster UFS 4.0 storage, available in 256GB, 512GB, and 1TB configurations. The speedier storage technology in the S24 Ultra allows quicker data access and smoother performance, especially when loading large files or apps.

One of the most significant differentiators between these two phones is their camera systems. Google has long been renowned for its computational photography. It includes a 50 MP wide lens, a 48 MP periscope telephoto lens with 5x optical zoom, and a 48 MP ultrawide lens. This combination allows the Pixel 9 Pro to capture stunning images in a variety of conditions, with features like multi-zone laser autofocus, Ultra-HDR, and Pixel Shift enhancing the overall photography experience. The phone also supports 8K video recording at 30fps, making it a powerful tool for videographers.

Samsung, however, has positioned the S24 Ultra as the ultimate camera phone. It features a quad-camera setup with a staggering 200 MP wide lens, a 50 MP periscope telephoto lens with 5x optical zoom, a 10 MP telephoto lens with 3x optical zoom, and a 12 MP ultrawide lens. This array of cameras allows the S24 Ultra to capture incredibly detailed images, whether you're zooming in on distant objects or taking wide-angle shots. The S24 Ultra also supports 8K video recording, but with additional frame rate options (24/30fps), giving users more flexibility when shooting high-resolution video. The front-facing camera on the S24 Ultra, while less powerful than the Pixel 9 Pro's 42 MP selfie camera, still offers solid performance with a 12 MP sensor that supports dual video calls and HDR10+.

Battery life is another critical aspect of these two phones' differences. The Pixel 9 Pro comes with a 4700 mAh battery, which supports 27W wired charging and 21W wireless charging with the Pixel Stand. With wired charging, the phone can charge up to 55% in 30 minutes, ensuring that users can quickly top up their battery during the day. The Pixel 9 Pro also supports reverse wireless charging, allowing it to charge other devices like earbuds.

The Samsung S24 Ultra, on the other hand, is equipped with a larger 5000 mAh battery, which offers longer battery life, especially during intensive use. It supports faster 45W wired charging, capable of reaching 65% in just 30 minutes, as well as 15W wireless charging and 4.5W reverse wireless charging. This makes the S24 Ultra better suited for users who need a device that can last all day on a single charge, even with heavy usage.

Regarding software, both devices run on Android 14, with Google offering its clean Pixel experience and Samsung providing its feature-rich One UI 6.1.1.

The Google Pixel 9 Pro and the Samsung Galaxy S24 Ultra are exceptional smartphones, each excelling in different areas. The Pixel 9 Pro is ideal for users who prioritize a compact design, advanced photography, and a pure Android experience. The Samsung S24 Ultra, with its larger display, more powerful processor, and additional productivity features, is better suited for those who need a versatile device that can handle everything from gaming to professional tasks.

pixel 9 pro vs iphone 15 pro

Last but not least: The iPhone. While not an Android device, it's worth comparing because both companies tend to copy patterns in terms of both their software and hardware.

With dimensions of 152.8 x 72 x 8.5 mm and a weight of 199 grams, the Pixel 9 Pro is designed to be both substantial and ergonomic. Its build quality reflects Google's commitment to premium materials, featuring a glass front and back protected by Corning Gorilla Glass Victus 2, and an aluminum frame that adds durability without compromising on aesthetics. The Pixel 9 Pro is also IP68 certified, making it dustproof and water-resistant up to 1.5 meters for 30 minutes.

In contrast, the iPhone 15 Pro, released in September 2023, showcases Apple's meticulous design philosophy. Slightly more compact than the Pixel, the iPhone 15 Pro measures 146.6 x 70.6 x 8.3 mm and weighs 187 grams, making it lighter and a touch smaller, which could appeal to users who prefer a more pocket-friendly device. The iPhone's build includes a titanium frame, a step up from the previous stainless steel, and a glass front and back made by Corning. This design provides robustness and gives the iPhone 15 Pro a unique feel, blending strength with lightweight construction. The device is also IP68 certified, but it extends its water resistance to depths of up to 6 meters for 30 minutes, offering a higher protection level than the Pixel 9 Pro.

Display technology is a crucial factor in a smartphone's appeal, and here, both Google and Apple have made significant strides. The Pixel 9 Pro features a 6.3-inch LTPO OLED display with a 1280 x 2856 pixels resolution, resulting in a sharp 495 ppi density. This screen supports HDR10+ and can reach an impressive peak brightness of 3000 nits, making it exceptionally bright and vibrant, even in direct sunlight. The 120Hz refresh rate ensures smooth scrolling and a responsive touch experience, which is especially beneficial for gaming and fast-paced content.

The iPhone 15 Pro, while slightly smaller with a 6.1-inch LTPO Super Retina XDR OLED display, also brings top-tier visual performance. Its resolution of 1179 x 2556 pixels delivers a pixel density of 461 ppi, slightly lower than the Pixel but still incredibly sharp. The iPhone's display supports HDR10, Dolby Vision, and achieves a peak brightness of 2000 nits in high-brightness mode (HBM), which is lower than the Pixel 9 Pro but still highly visible under most lighting conditions. Apple's focus on color accuracy and brightness consistency across its devices means the iPhone 15 Pro offers one of the best displays available, even if it doesn't reach the extreme brightness of the Pixel 9 Pro.

Under the hood, the Pixel 9 Pro is powered by Google's Tensor G4 chipset, a 4nm octa-core processor that includes a Cortex-X4 core clocked at 3.1 GHz, three Cortex-A720 cores at 2.6 GHz, and four Cortex-A520 cores at 1.92 GHz. This setup ensures that the Pixel 9 Pro can easily handle the most demanding tasks, from gaming to intensive multitasking. The Mali-G715 MC7 GPU complements the CPU, providing robust graphics performance that will appeal to gamers and those who use their phone for media consumption.

The iPhone 15 Pro, on the other hand, is equipped with Apple's A17 Pro chipset, built on a 3nm process. This chip features a hexa-core CPU with two high-performance cores clocked at 3.78 GHz and four efficiency cores at 2.11 GHz. The A17 Pro, coupled with a 6-core Apple GPU, delivers exceptional performance, particularly in power efficiency and thermal management. This makes the iPhone 15 Pro fast and capable of maintaining performance over extended periods without overheating, a key advantage in sustained workloads or gaming sessions.

Memory and storage options reflect Google's and Apple's different philosophies. The Pixel 9 Pro comes with 16GB of RAM across all its storage variants, which include 128GB, 256GB, 512GB, and 1TB options. This large amount of RAM ensures that the Pixel can handle multiple apps running simultaneously without any slowdown, making it ideal for power users who demand high performance from their device.

In contrast, the iPhone 15 Pro is more conservative with its 8GB of RAM, paired with storage options that mirror those of the Pixel: 128GB, 256GB, 512GB, and 1TB. While 8GB of RAM might seem less on paper, Apple's iOS is highly optimized, and this amount of memory is more than sufficient for the smooth operation of the device, even during heavy multitasking. The use of NVMe storage in the iPhone also contributes to its fast performance, allowing for quick data access and app loading times.

Camera capabilities are often a major selling point for smartphones, and both the Pixel 9 Pro and iPhone 15 Pro deliver exceptional results, albeit in different ways. The Pixel 9 Pro features a triple-camera setup on the rear, including a 50 MP wide lens, a 48 MP periscope telephoto lens with 5x optical zoom, and a 48 MP ultrawide lens. This array is designed to cover a wide range of photographic scenarios, from expansive landscapes to detailed close-ups, with Google's software enhancements like Pixel Shift, Ultra-HDR, and Zoom Enhance further improving the quality of photos and videos. The front-facing camera is a standout 42 MP sensor, which is particularly impressive for selfies and video calls, offering high levels of detail and clarity.

Apple, known for its strong emphasis on photography, equips the iPhone 15 Pro with a slightly different camera setup. The rear camera system includes a 48 MP wide lens, a 12 MP telephoto lens with 3x optical zoom, and a 12 MP ultrawide lens. The iPhone also includes a TOF 3D LiDAR scanner for enhanced depth sensing, improving photography, and augmented reality applications. While the iPhone's telephoto capabilities are less powerful than the Pixel's, Apple's computational photography, including features like Smart HDR and Deep Fusion, ensures that photos are consistently excellent across various conditions. The front-facing camera on the iPhone 15 Pro is a 12 MP sensor, which, while lower in resolution than the Pixel's, is highly capable, especially with its inclusion of sensor-shift optical image stabilization (OIS) and support for 4K video recording.

Battery life and charging options are crucial factors for many users. The Pixel 9 Pro comes with a 4700 mAh battery, supporting 27W wired charging, 21W wireless charging with the Pixel Stand, and reverse wireless charging. This battery capacity, combined with Google's software optimizations, ensures that the Pixel can last through a full day of use, even with heavy applications. The fast charging capabilities mean that users can quickly top up their battery, reaching 55% in just 30 minutes with wired charging.

The iPhone 15 Pro, with its smaller 3274 mAh battery, offers slightly less battery life, but Apple's A17 Pro chipset is incredibly power-efficient, helping to extend the device's endurance. The iPhone supports 50% charge in 30 minutes using wired charging (PD2.0), 15W wireless charging via MagSafe, and 15W wireless charging with Qi2, provided the device is updated to iOS 17.2. Additionally, the iPhone offers 4.5W reverse wired charging, a feature that can be handy for charging smaller accessories on the go.

Regarding software, the Pixel 9 Pro runs on Android 14, with Google promising up to seven major Android upgrades, ensuring long-term support and access to the latest features. The iPhone 15 Pro runs on iOS 17, which is upgradable to future versions, including iOS 18. Apple's ecosystem is known for its seamless integration across devices, which might appeal to users already invested in other Apple products like the iPad or MacBook.

The Pixel 9 Pro and iPhone 15 Pro are exceptional smartphones, each offering a unique blend of features that cater to different user preferences. The Pixel 9 Pro is ideal for users who prioritize camera versatility, display brightness, and the customizability of Android. The iPhone 15 Pro, with its compact design, advanced chipset, and deep integration with Apple's ecosystem, is better suited for users who value efficiency, security, and a seamless experience across multiple devices.

2 /
getting started

setup

THE SETUP IS PRETTY INTUITIVE, but there are still screens that might confuse you a little. If you are a self-starter and like just try things, then skip to the next section on the main UI elements of Android. If you want a more thorough walk-through, then read away!

Google knows you want to get started using your phone, so they've made the process pretty quick; most people will spend about 5 or 10 minutes.

The first thing you'll see is the "Hi there" screen; you could technically make an emergency call on this screen, but I don't recommend it unless it's really an emergency—this isn't a "hey, mom, I'll be late" emergency...this is a direct to emergency responders "I've fallen and can't get up" sort of call. When you are ready to get started, tap the blue "Start" button.

You have two options on the next screen: connect to wi-fi so you can start a "SIM-free" setup or insert your SIM card.

If you add a SIM card you can skip all of the next steps. If you are doing SIM-Free, then tap "Start SIM-free setup instead." The next screen explains SIM-free; SIM-free is exactly what it sounds like, but it's not supported by all carriers. If your carrier supports it, then I'd recommend doing it, as everything will be stored online vs. on a card that can be easily scratched and damaged. Tap the blue "Next" to begin.

SIM-free setup

If your mobile network uses SIM-free setup, you'll get calls, texts, and data by downloading an eSIM instead of inserting a SIM card.

The next screen prompts you to select your wi-fi network. This is followed by an update screen. It should take about a minute to get the latest update. When it's done, you'll see the "Copy apps & data" screen.

Mastering the Pixel 9 and Pixel 9 Pro

Copy apps & data

You can choose to transfer your apps, photos, contacts, Google Account, and more.

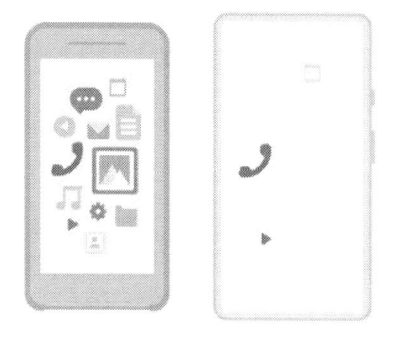

Copy apps and data is pretty resourceful. It will let you copy everything from your old phone so there's not as much to do on your new one—it works with both iPhone (through a special adaptor) and Android. It's not perfect—especially with the iPhone—but it will save you time. If you are coming from a previous generation Android phone, you can also do this without a cord by using your login. If you want to skip it and start from scratch, then select "Don't copy" in the lower left corner.

Scott La Counte

Find your old phone's cable

Use a cable that fits your old phone. This is usually the cable used for charging.

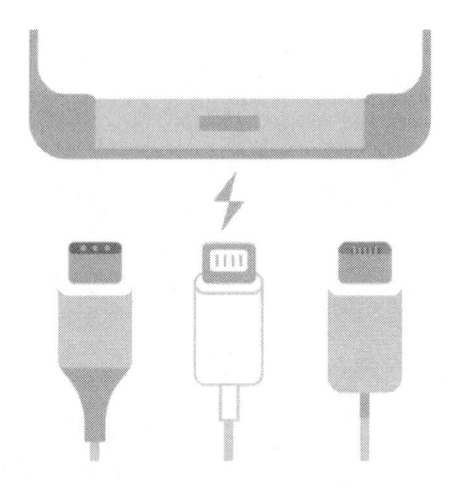

Insert cable into your old phone

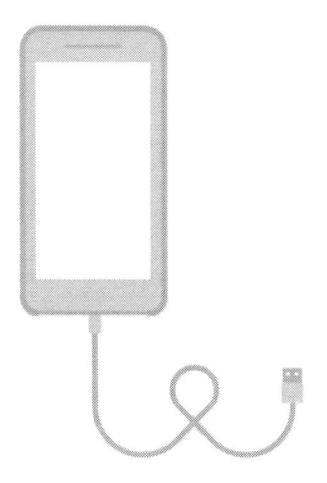

Next, sign in to your Google Account (the one you use the check email usually—unless you don't use Gmail). If you don't have a Google Account, then click the option to create it.

Scott La Counte

Google
Sign in
with your Google Account. Learn more

Email or phone

Forgot email?

Create account

Once you hit "next" and "sign in," you'll get a bunch of legal stuff. It's basically saying Google's not responsible for anything. Agree to it or you just bought yourself a very expensive brick. You'll see a lot of these legal screens, so either put on your reading glasses and settle in for a very long night, or just agree to them.

Google Services is the next screen. This is giving the phone permission to use features on the phone (like the fingerprint scanner, location services to see where you are at, send Google and developers crash reports, and backup your phone to the Google Drive). I recommend selecting all of them. If you are worried about privacy, I'll show you some adjustments you can make later. I should also note: if you turn them off here, you can turn them back on later.

Device maintenance

Send usage and diagnostic data ⌄

Help improve your Android experience by automatically sending diagnostic, device, and app usage data to Google. This will help battery life, system and app stability, and other improvements. Some aggregate data will also help Google apps and partners, such as Android developers. If your additional Web & App Activity setting is turned on, this data may be saved to your Google Account.

Install updates & apps ⌄

By continuing, you agree that this device may also automatically download and install updates and apps from Google, your carrier, and your device's manufacturer, possibly using cellular data. Some of these apps may offer in-app purchases.

Tap "Accept" to confirm your selection of these Google services settings.

[Accept]

Next is yet another reminder that you can't blame Google for anything. They really want you to understand this. That way if the phone explodes in your hand, it's obviously your fault!

Additional legal terms

By clicking "I accept," you agree to the Google Terms of Service and the Google Device Arbitration Agreement.
Note: The Google Privacy Policy describes how your data is handled.

All disputes regarding your Google device will be resolved through **binding arbitration** on an individual, non-class basis, as described in the Google Device Arbitration Agreement, unless you opt out by following the instructions in that Agreement.

Next, it's time to start setting up your phone. What was all that other stuff? That was your account. First up to bat: your screen lock. This is basically so if someone steals or finds your phone, they can't open it unless they know your password.

Set screen lock

For security, set PIN

PIN must be at least 4 digits

Screen lock options

If you tap on "Screen lock options" you will see even more options. The unlock can be a pattern (e.g. move in the shape of a seven), it can be a word, or it could be a number (but don't use your bank pin number!). You can also skip adding a pin and have your phone always unlocked.

The next screen will ask you for a pin. If you tap "Screen lock options" you can also add a pattern. It's all a preference. My only advice is not to use a pin you use somewhere else (like a bank pin) or an easy pin (like 1234).

Once you hit "Next," and then reenter the pin to confirm it.

You'll also have the option for adding a fingerprint to unlock your phone. Unlike a lot of phones, the Pixels fingerprint sensor is on the screen itself. Pretty cool right? Here's a nugget of advice, however. If you are like me, you'll probably put a screen protector over it so there's more protection if it falls. That's going to be problematic for your sensor until you update it—so if you are finding it's not working, then update the Android software (I'll show you how later) and see if that fixes it.

Set up Fingerprint Unlock

Use your fingerprint to unlock your phone or verify it's you, like when you sign in to apps or approve a purchase.

How it works

Fingerprint Unlock creates a unique model of your fingerprint to verify it's

More

Adding a finger print is pretty simple. The phone will tell you exactly where your finger should go. Just tap your finger to the screen where shown. That's it! You can add one finger or several. You can also add other people's fingers—so if you have someone who you give permission to use your phone, then you can add them as well.

Scott La Counte

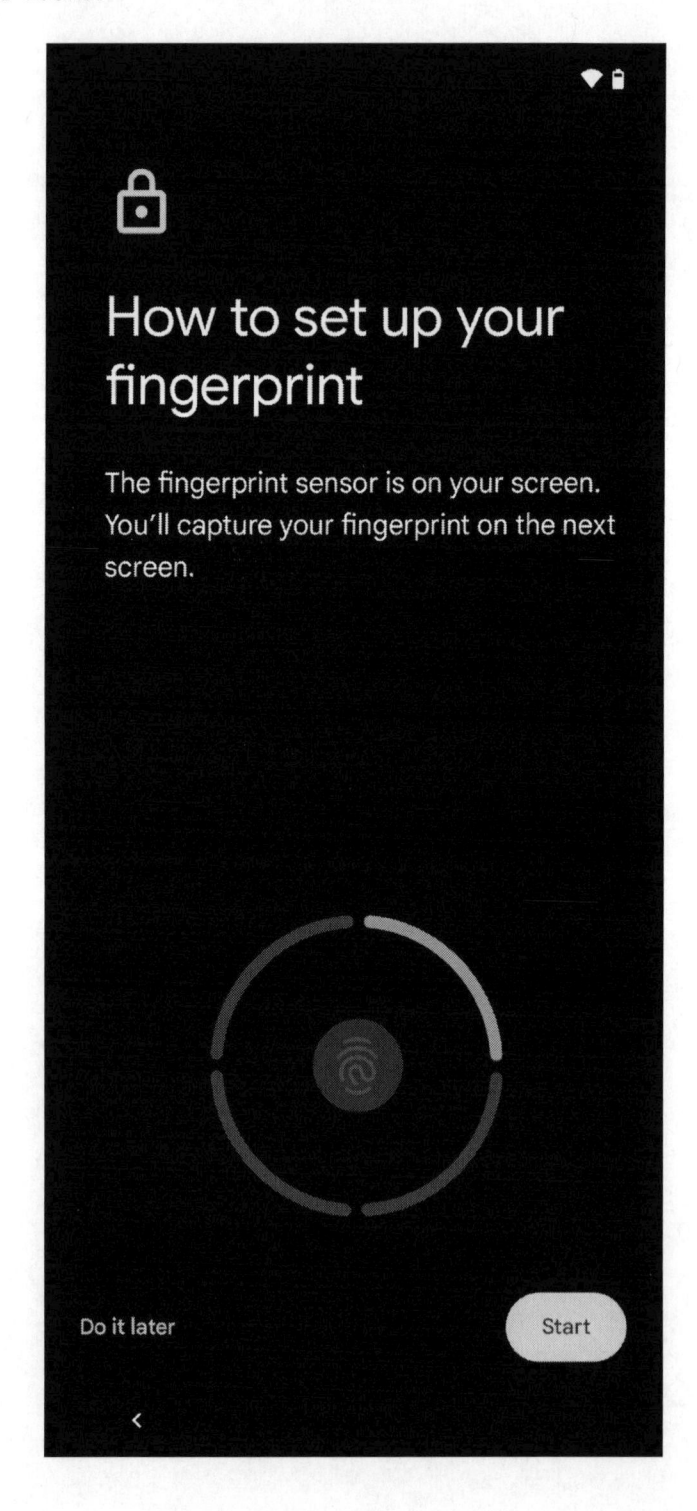

Just tap Add Another at the end of the setup if you want to add more.

Scott La Counte

Mastering the Pixel 9 and Pixel 9 Pro

New to Pixel 7 is the ability to unlock with your face; this is something that's been missing sense the Pixel 4.

Configuring Google Assistant is next. Google Assistant is the Google equivalent of Siri. You can tap "Leave & get reminder" but it's very quick to do, so it's best to just get it out of the way.

Make Pixel uniquely yours

Keep going to set up your Google Assistant, change your wallpaper, and more. Or, leave now and finish later.

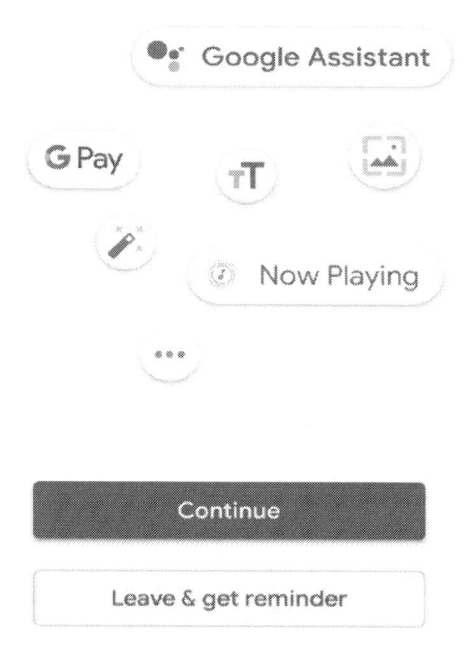

Once you agree to the terms, you are ready to go. You'll be asked a few

49

questions (unless you have a Google Home and Google already knows your voice).

You are just about done! The "Anything else?" screen is your last chance to add in settings before finishing the set up—and remember: you can change all this later. So if you don't want to do it now, you always can do it later. The one thing I will point out is "Add another email account"; if you are using this phone at work, then it's a good idea to add in your work email here.

Anything else?

Set up a few more things now, or find them later in Settings

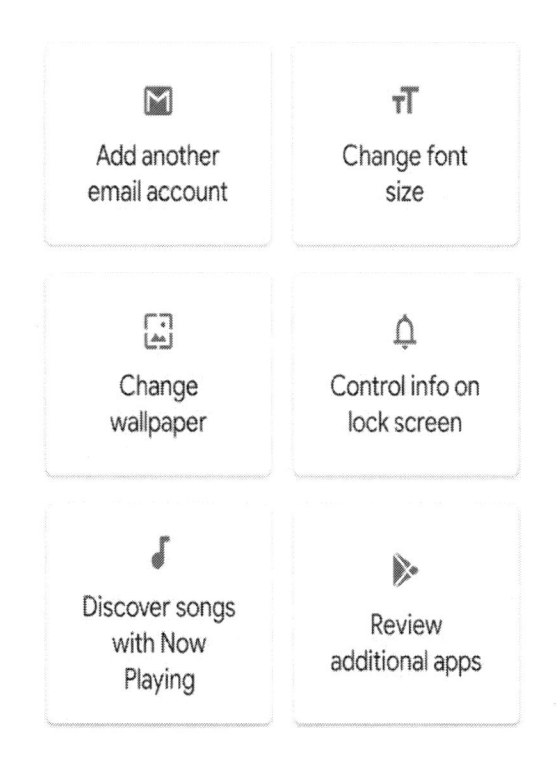

- Add another email account
- Change font size
- Change wallpaper
- Control info on lock screen
- Discover songs with Now Playing
- Review additional apps

No thanks

The last screen is asking if you'd like to get tip emails from Google about how to use your phone. When you are first getting started, these emails are helpful. They don't come very often. If you want to turn it on, then just toggle the "sign up" button to on (it will turn blue—or be blue if it's already checked).

More tips & tricks

For support, updates, and more, go to Settings > Support

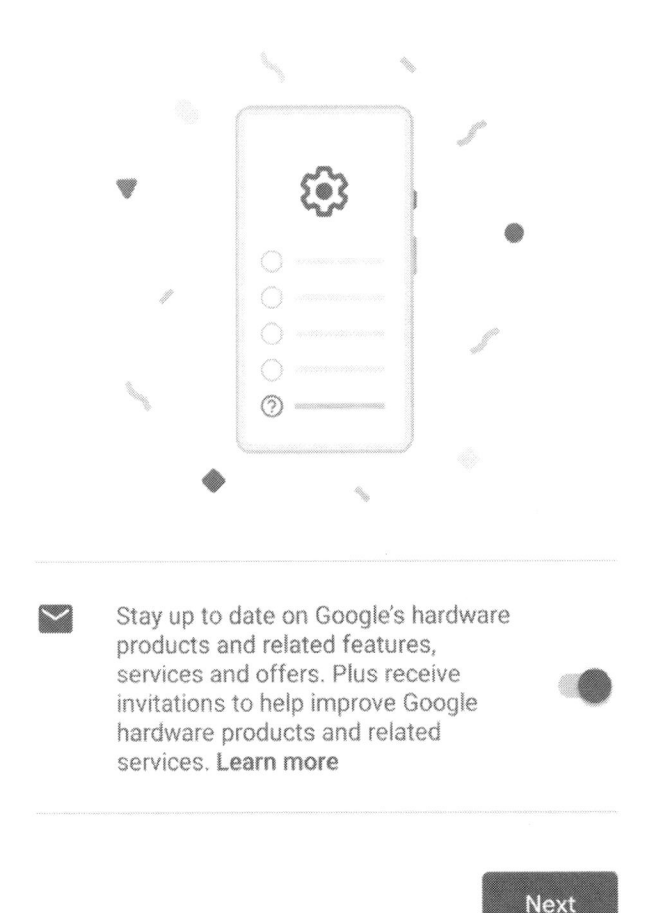

Stay up to date on Google's hardware products and related features, services and offers. Plus receive invitations to help improve Google hardware products and related services. **Learn more**

Next

After a few seconds, a screen will appear that says, "Go Home." Kind of sounds like the phone is telling you that you didn't pass the setup and now must go home empty handed.

Scott La Counte

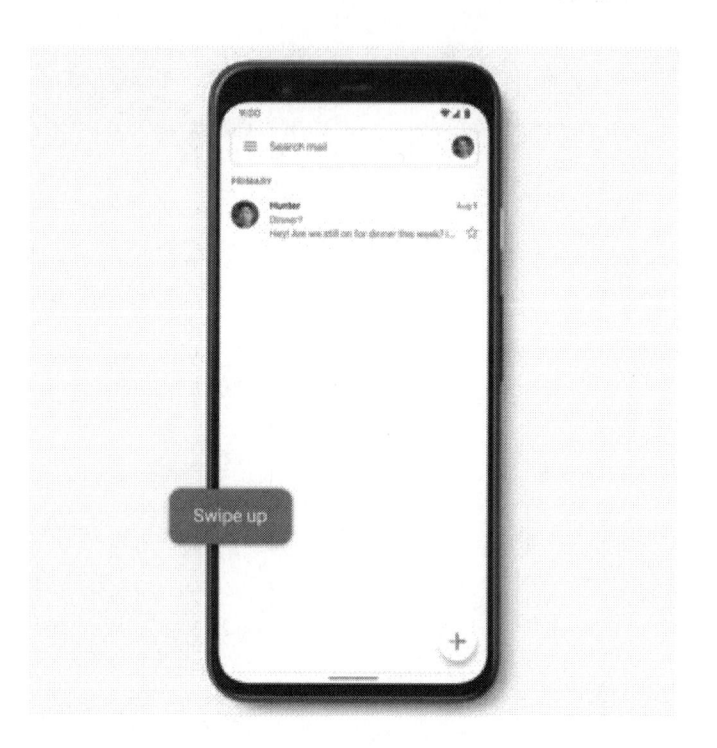

Go Home

Swipe up from the bottom of your screen. This gesture always takes you to the Home screen.

Next

54

Don't worry! It's just telling you to go to the Home screen because you are finally done. These final screens are short tutorials that will give you a couple tips for how the phone works.

After a few tips, you'll see the "All set!" screen, which is the final screen. You are finally done!

Swipe up and you will see your Home screen. You are finally ready to use your phone!

finding your way around

People come to the Pixel from all sorts of different places: iPhone, other Android phone, flip phone, two styrofoam cups tied together with string. This next section is a crash course in the interface. If you've used Android before, then it might seem a little simple, so skip ahead if you already know all of this.

If any of this seems a little rushed, there's good reason: it is! We'll cover these points in more detail later. This is just a quick starter / reference.

On the bottom of your screen is the shortcut bar—you'll be spending a lot of time here; you can add whatever you want to this area, but these are the apps Google thinks you'll use most—and, with the exception of the Play Store, they are probably right. Depending on the settings you've picked and the phone you have, it may or may not look different. It could show four apps in a row instead of six, for example.

So, what are these? Real quick, these are as follows:

- **Phone**: Do you want to take a wild guess what the phone button does? If you said brings you an ice cream, then maybe you aren't cut out for a phone. But if you said something along the lines of "It launches an app to call people" then you'll have no problem at all with your new device. Surprise, surprise: this pricey gadget that plays games, takes pictures, and keeps you up to date on political ramblings on social media does one more interesting thing: it calls people!
- **Message**: Message might be a little more open-ended than "Phone"; that could mean email message, text messages, messages you keep getting on your bathroom mirror to put the toilet seat down. In this case, it means "text messages" (but really —put that toilet seat down...you aren't doing anyone any favors).

57

This is the app you'll use whenever you want to text cute pictures of cats.
- **Play Store**: Anything with the word "Play" in the title must be fun, right?! This app is what you'll use to download all those fun apps you always hear about.
- **Chrome**: Whenever you want to surf the Internet, you'll use Chrome. There are actually several apps that do the same thing—like Firefox and Opera—but I recommend Chrome until you are comfortable with your phone. Personally, I think it's the best app for searching the Internet, but you'll soon learn that most things on the phone are about preference, and you may find another Internet browser that suits your needs more.
- **Camera**: This apps opens pictures of vintage cameras…just kidding! It's how you take pictures on your phone. You use this same app for videos as well.

Next to the shortcut bar, the area you'll use the most is the notification bar. This is where you'll get, you guessed it, notifications! What's a notification? That's any kind of notice you have elected to receive. A few examples: text message alerts, email alerts, amber alerts, and apps that have updates.

Mastering the Pixel 9 and Pixel 9 Pro

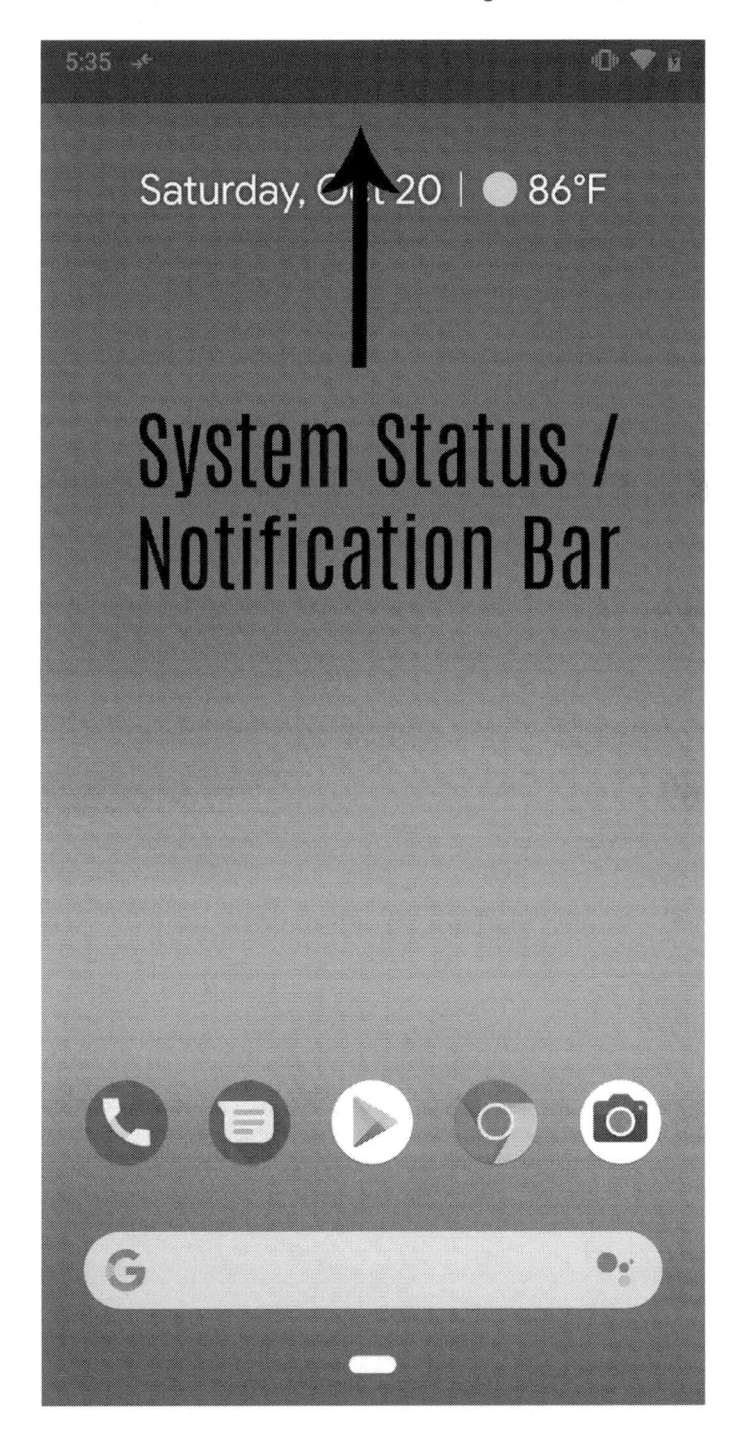

System Status / Notification Bar

When you drag your finger down from the notification bar, you'll get a list of several settings that you can adjust. Press and hold any of these options and you'll open an app with even more options.

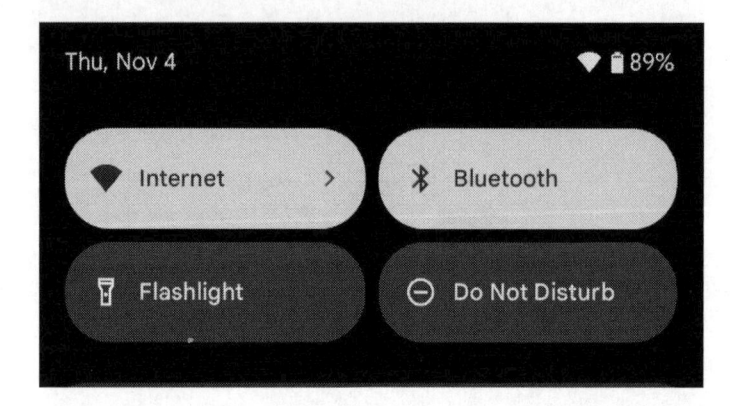

From right to left these are the options you can change or use:

- Wi-fi
- Bluetooth
- Do not disturb
- Flashlight

If you continue dragging down, this thin menu expands and there are a few more options.

Mastering the Pixel 9 and Pixel 9 Pro

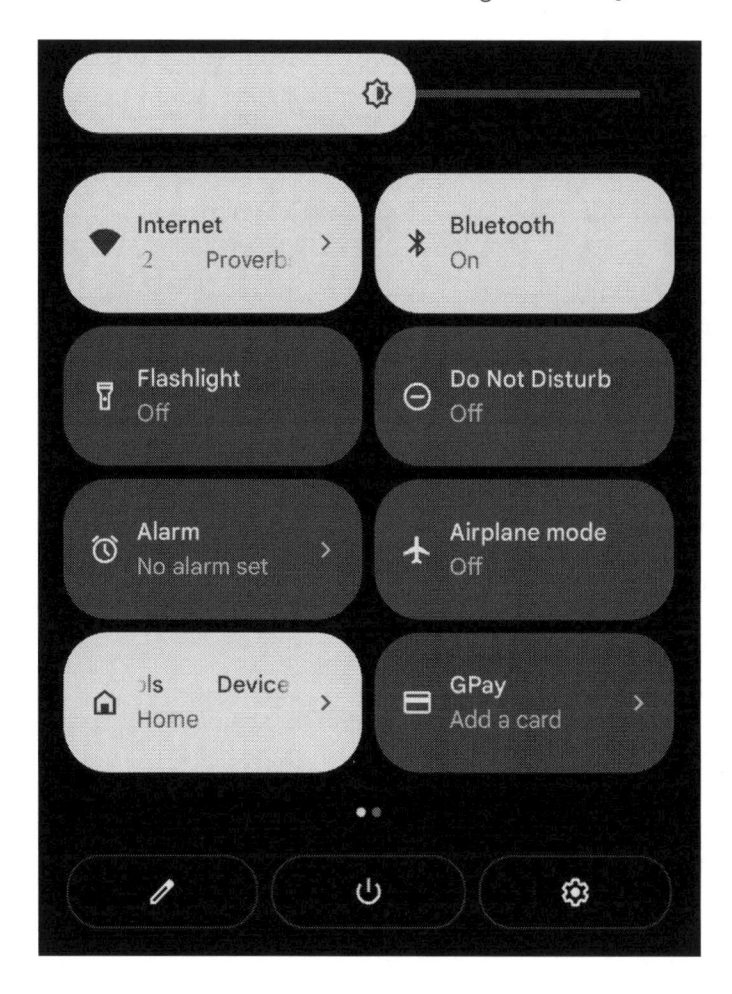

The first is at the top of the screen—it's the slider, and it makes your device brighter or dimmer depending on which way you drag it.

You can slide your finger to see more options:

- Auto-Rotate – Locks (unlocks) the device from rotating
- Battery Saver – Puts the device in a low energy mode for extended battery life, but not as great processing power.
- Screen cast – Beams the screen to another device—like a Google TV.
- Screen Record – Screen recording used to be something you needed a special app for; Android 11 brought native recording. So

61

you can record what you are doing on your screen and share it with someone else. It's great for tutorial videos. You are also able to use your phone's microphone to narrate with your voice.
- Nearby share
- Camera / Mic Disable – Quickly turn off your camera or mic.

Near the bottom on the left, is a little pencil edit button. That let's you reorganize what options are shown where.

← **Edit**　　　　　　　　　　⋮

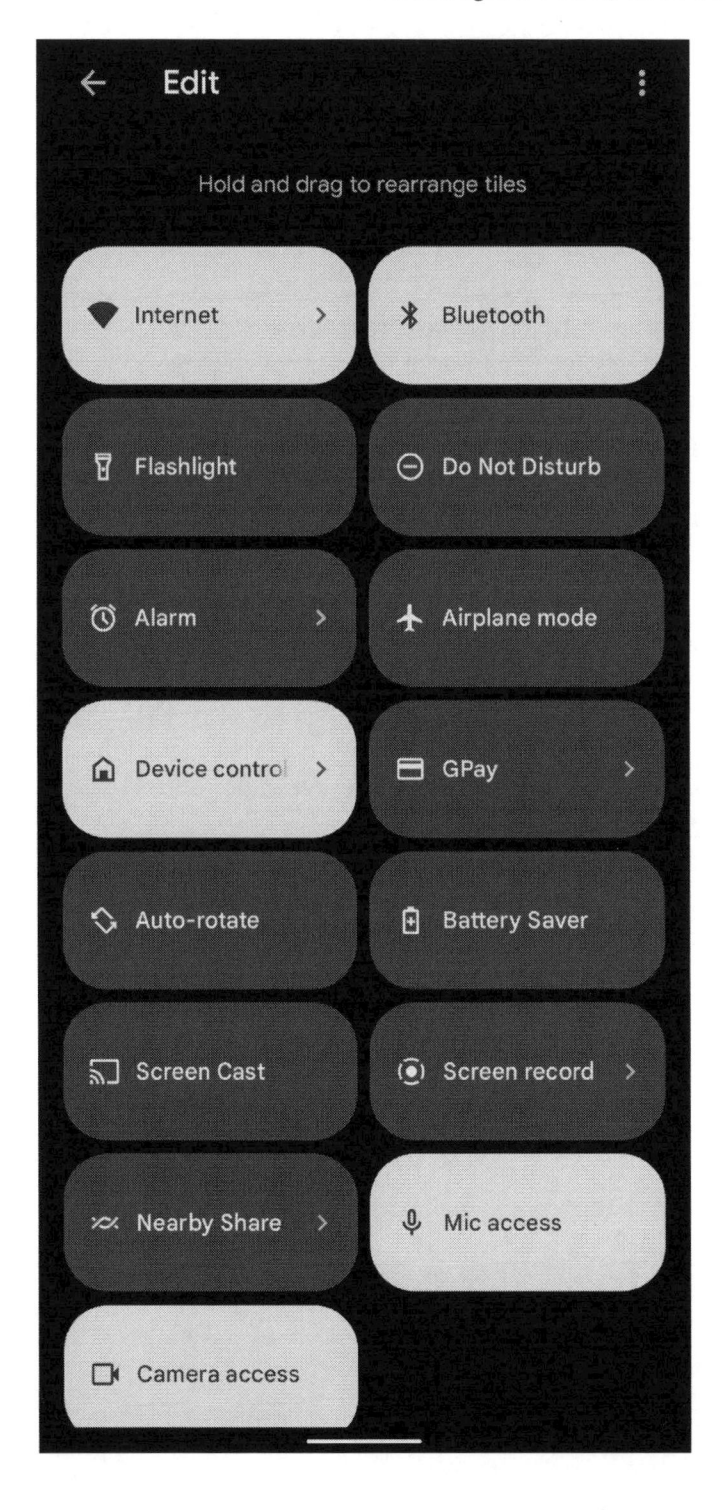

Hold and drag to rearrange tiles

◆ Internet >	✱ Bluetooth
🔦 Flashlight	⊖ Do Not Disturb
⏰ Alarm >	✈ Airplane mode
🏠 Device control >	💳 GPay >
⟲ Auto-rotate	🔋 Battery Saver
📡 Screen Cast	⦿ Screen record >
⤨ Nearby Share >	🎤 Mic access
📷 Camera access	

Scroll a little more and you'll see even more quick settings that you can add to the notification bar. Among them:

- **Data** – Tapping this turns your data on and off, which is handy if you are running low on data and don't want to be charged extra for it.
- **Night light** - This is a special mode that dims your screen and makes the screen appropriate for reading in dark settings.
- **Battery share** – when you press this, you can use your device like a wireless charger. What does that mean? Let's say your friend has an iPhone with wireless charging and they're almost out of battery. You can press this, then hold their phone against yours and share your battery wirelessly with them.

Something else that's pretty cool on this notification area: you can see a history of notifications.

If you get a lot of notifications, you probably have accidentally dismissed something that you didn't mean to. Now you can see what it was.

To use it, go to the bottom of all your notifications, then select "Manage."

6:32

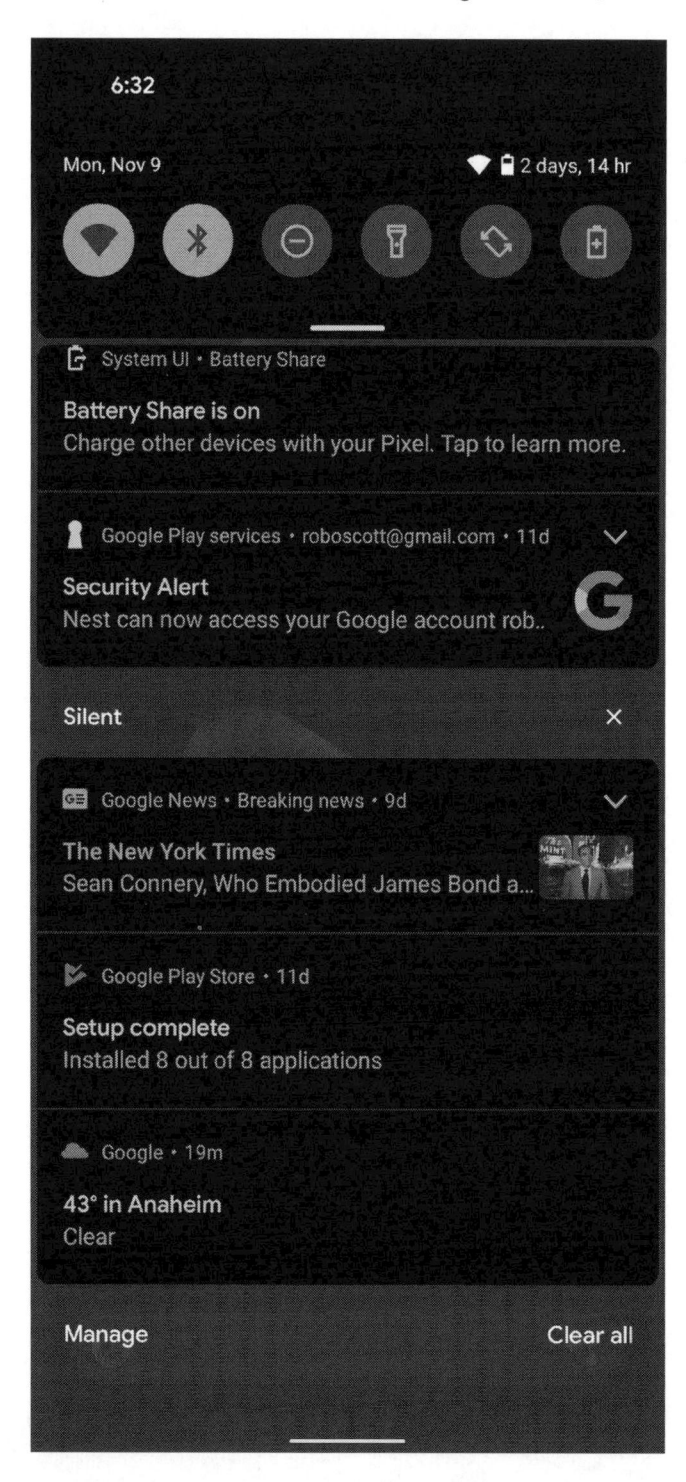

Mon, Nov 9   2 days, 14 hr

System UI • Battery Share
Battery Share is on
Charge other devices with your Pixel. Tap to learn more.

Google Play services • roboscott@gmail.com • 11d
Security Alert
Nest can now access your Google account rob..

Silent   ✕

Google News • Breaking news • 9d
The New York Times
Sean Connery, Who Embodied James Bond a...

Google Play Store • 11d
Setup complete
Installed 8 out of 8 applications

Google • 19m
43° in Anaheim
Clear

Manage   Clear all

From here, toggle "Use notification history" to on.

Mastering the Pixel 9 and Pixel 9 Pro

Notification history

Use notification history

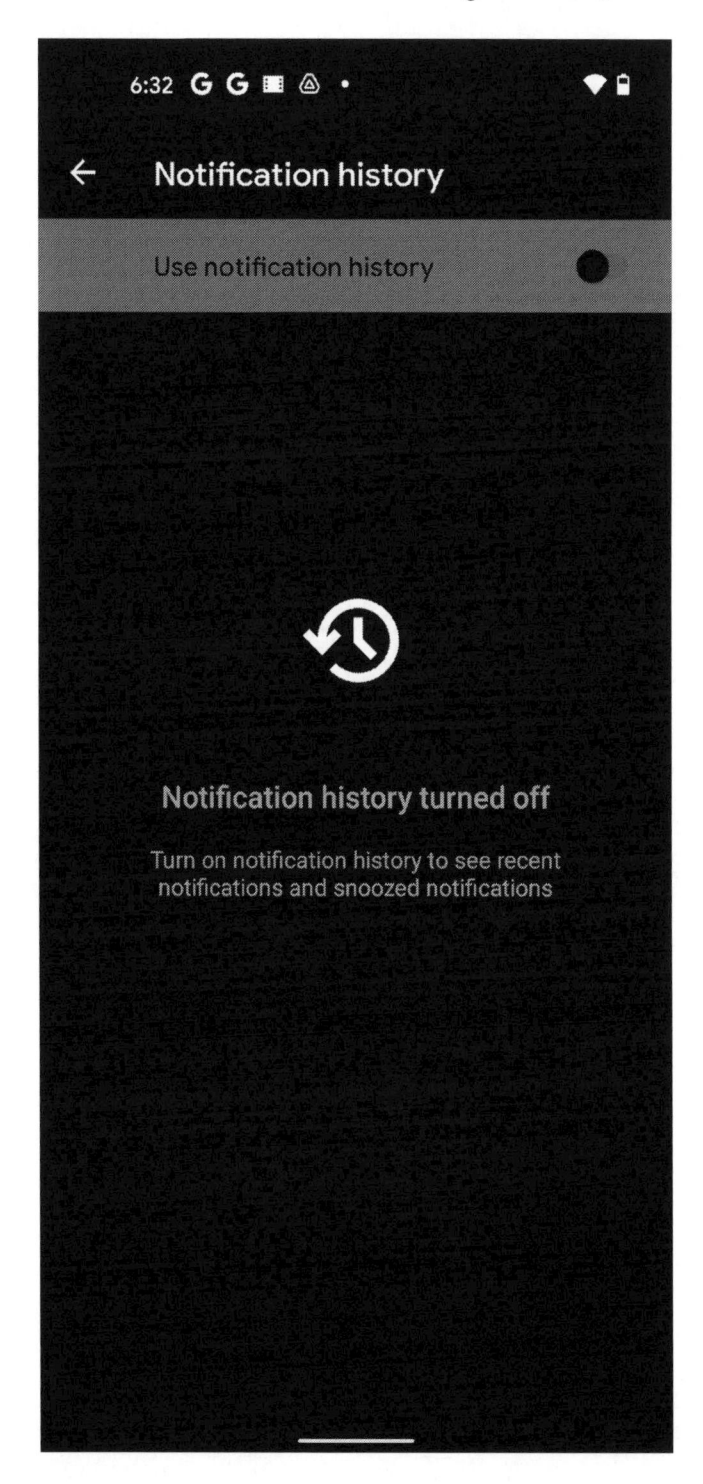

Notification history turned off

Turn on notification history to see recent notifications and snoozed notifications

Now when you go back to that same area "Manage" is replaced with "History."

6:32

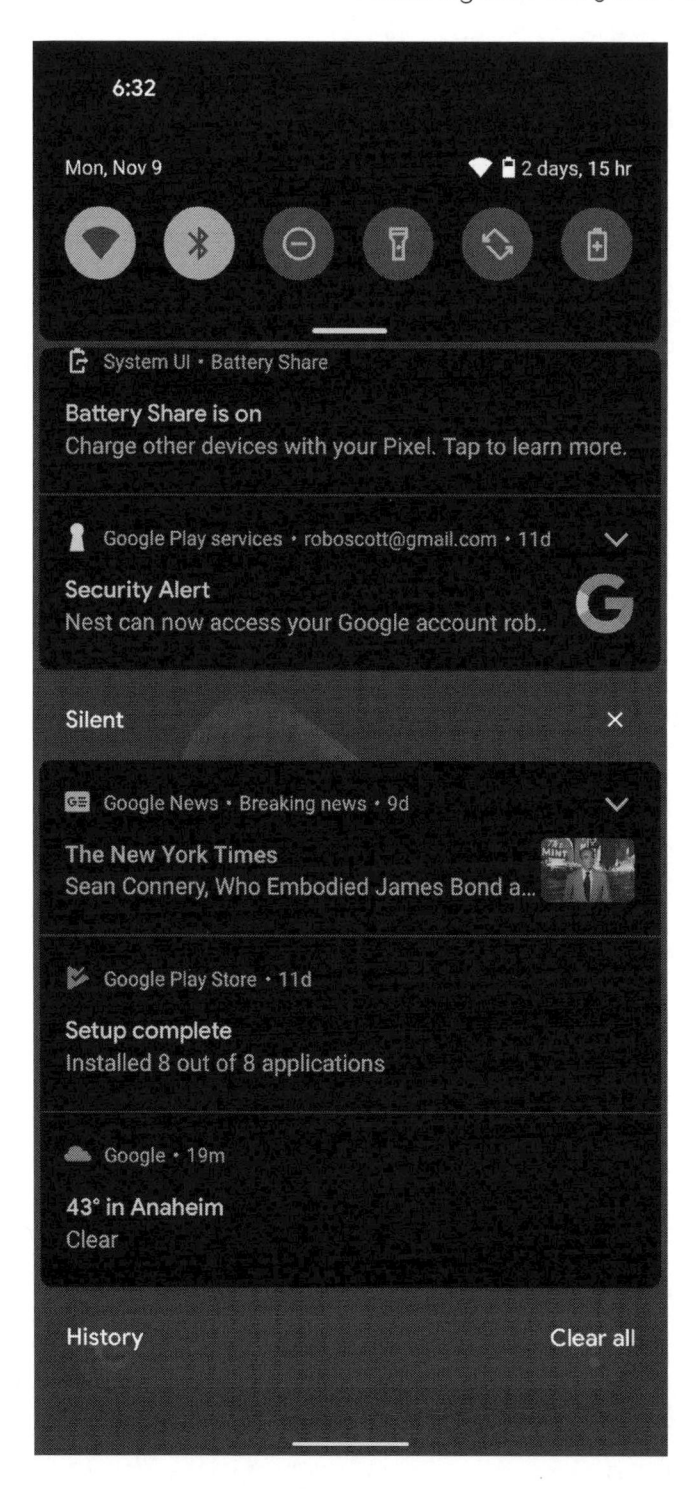

Mon, Nov 9   ▼ 🔋 2 days, 15 hr

📇 System UI • Battery Share

Battery Share is on
Charge other devices with your Pixel. Tap to learn more.

👤 Google Play services • roboscott@gmail.com • 11d

Security Alert
Nest can now access your Google account rob..

Silent   ✕

Google News • Breaking news • 9d

The New York Times
Sean Connery, Who Embodied James Bond a...

▶ Google Play Store • 11d

Setup complete
Installed 8 out of 8 applications

☁ Google • 19m

43° in Anaheim
Clear

History   Clear all

feeling home-less?

You may have noticed something that seems important missing from your phone: a Home button. On older phones, this was a critical button that gets you to the Home screen whenever you push it.

How on Earth do you get Home without a Home button?! Easy. Are you ready? Swipe up. That's it!

If you've used any Apple device, then you might know a thing or two about Siri. She's the assistant that "sometimes" works; Google has its own version of Siri and it's called Google Assistant. The names not quite as creative as Siri, but many say it works better. I'll let you be the judge of that.

To get to the Google Assistant from anywhere, just say "Ok, Google." If you are on the Home screen, then there's also a Google Assistant widget. This little bar does more than make appointments and get your information—it's also a global search. What does that mean? It means you can type in anything you want to know, and it will search both the Internet and your phone. If it's a contact in your phone, then it will get you that. But if it's the opening hours for the Museum of Strange then it will search the Internet—it will also give you a map of the location and the phone number.

Mastering the Pixel 9 and Pixel 9 Pro

Google Search / Assistant

get around on your pixel phone

When it comes to getting around your Pixel, learning how to use gestures will be the quickest, most effective method. You can change some of the gesture options by going to the Settings app, then System > Gestures > System navigation.

The most important gesture is how to get back to the Home screen—there are no buttons after all. That's the easiest one to remember: swipe up from the bottom of the screen.

When you are on an Internet page, you can swipe from the left or right edge of the screen to go backwards or forwards.

To select text, tap and hold over the text, then lift your finger when it responds.

Multitasking

Those are the easy gestures to remember; if you want to move around quickly, however, you need to know the two big multitask gestures, which help you switch between apps.

The first is to see your open apps. To do this, swipe up like you're going to the Home screen, but keep going until about the middle of the screen and then stop and lift your finger—don't make a quick swipe-up gesture like you would when going Home. This will show you previews of all of your open apps, and you can swipe between them. Tap the one you want to open.

Mastering the Pixel 9 and Pixel 9 Pro

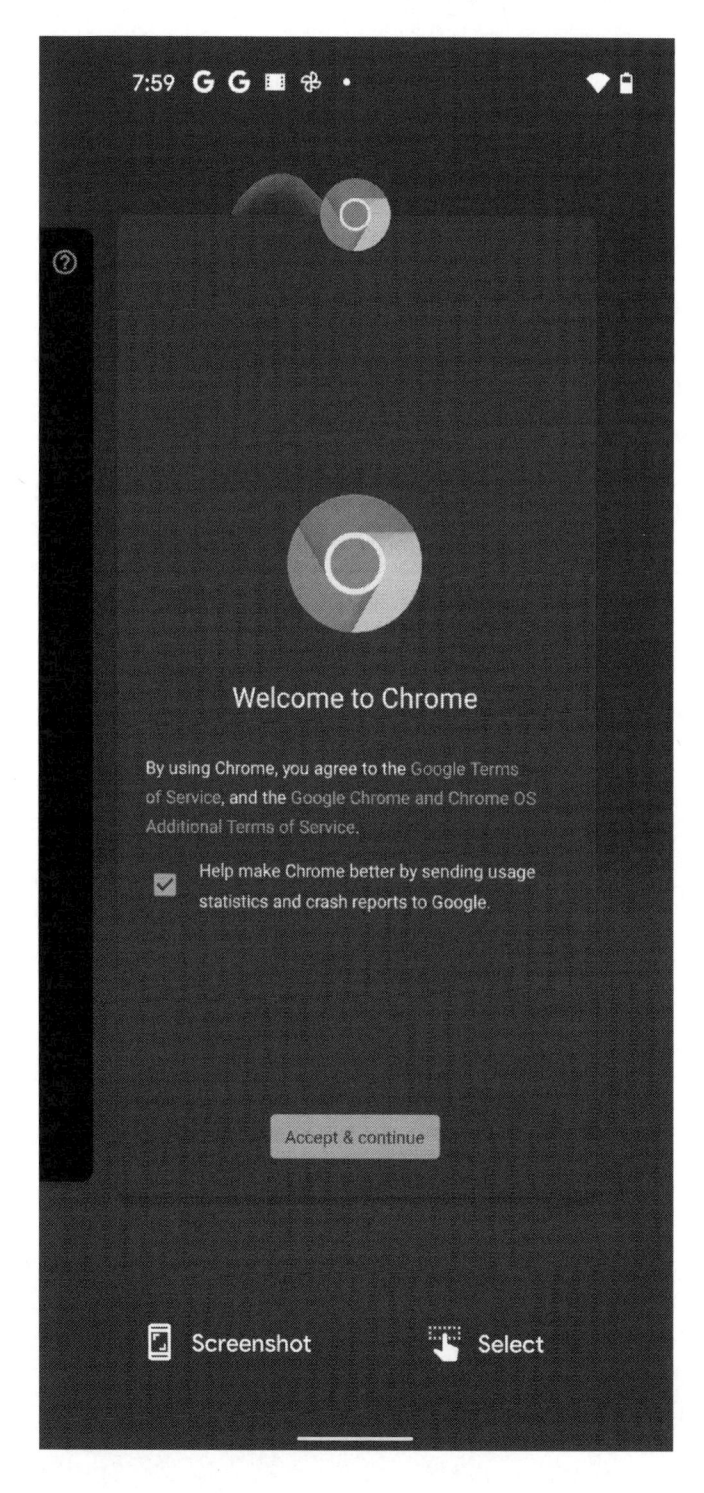

The quickest way to switch back and forth between two or three apps, however, is to swipe from left to right along the bottom edge of the screen. This swipes between apps in the order that you have used them.

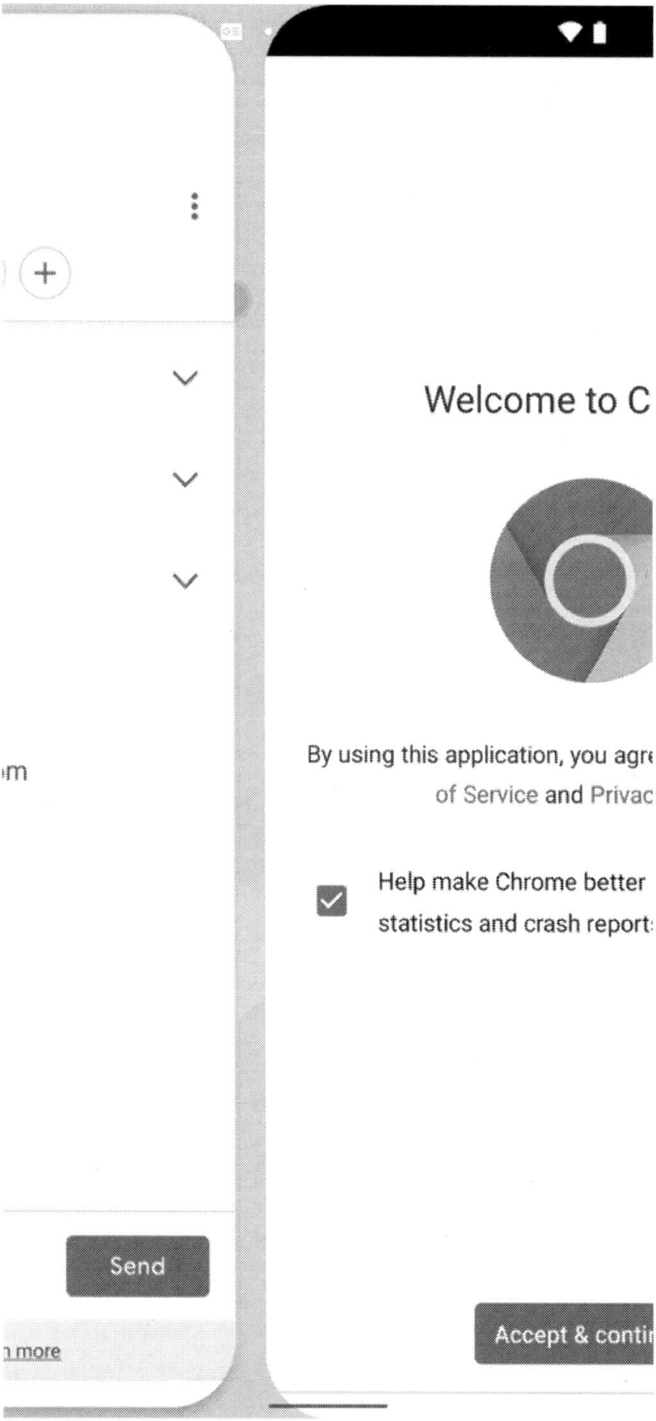
Welcome to C
By using this application, you agr
of Service and Privac
Help make Chrome better
statistics and crash report
Send
Accept & conti
more

Zoom

Need to see text bigger? There are two ways to do that. Note: this works on many, but not all apps.

The first way is to pinch to zoom.

7:12

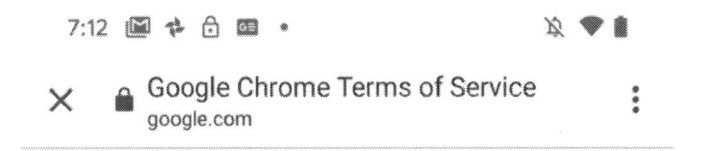

Google Chrome Terms of Service
google.com

r with the Additic
 between you an
es. It is importan
Collectively, this l
s".

etween what the
al Terms say, ther
elation to that Se

The second way is to double tap on the text.

Rotate

You probably have noticed if you rotate your phone, it rotates the screen. What if you don't want to rotate the entire screen? You can turn that off very easily. Swipe down and then tap the "arrows" button to enable or disable it.

3 /
the ridiculously simple overview of all the things you should know

making pretty screens

IF YOU'VE USED an iPhone or iPad, then you may notice the screen looks a little...bare. There's literally nothing on it. Maybe you like that. If so, then good for you! Skip ahead. If you want to decorate that screen with shortcuts and widgets, then read on. Since Android 12 made things more about you than ever before, prepare to have more control than ever before!

Adding Shortcuts

Any app you want on this screen, just find it, and then press and hold; when a menu comes up, drag it upward until the screen appears and move it to where you want it to go. You can also drag it to new screens.

To remove an app from a screen, tap and hold, then drag it upward to the "Remove" text that appears when you move it up. When it's there, let go.

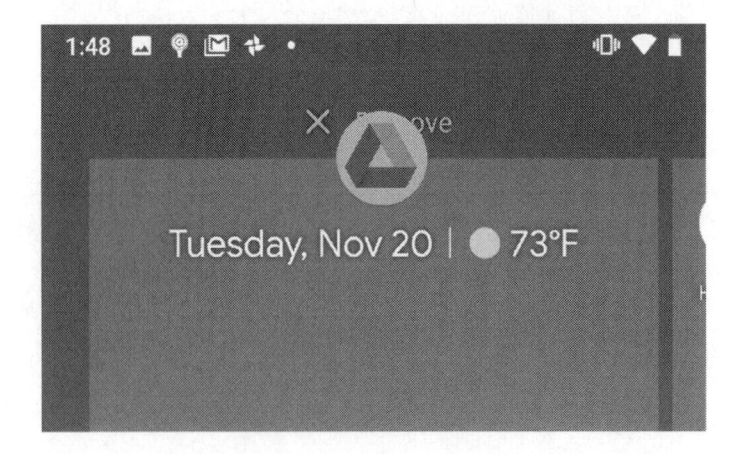

Widgets

Shortcuts are nice, but widgets are better. Widgets are sort of like mini-programs that run on your screen. A common widget people put on their screen is the weather forecast. Throughout the day the widget will update automatically with up-to-date info.

To add a widget, go to the screen you want to add it to and tap and hold until the menu comes up.

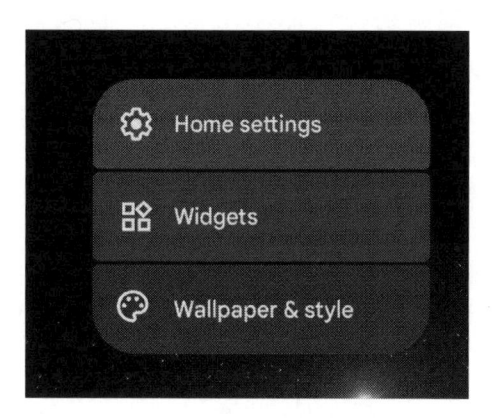

Select "Widgets." This opens up a widget library—it's like a mini app store.

Scott La Counte

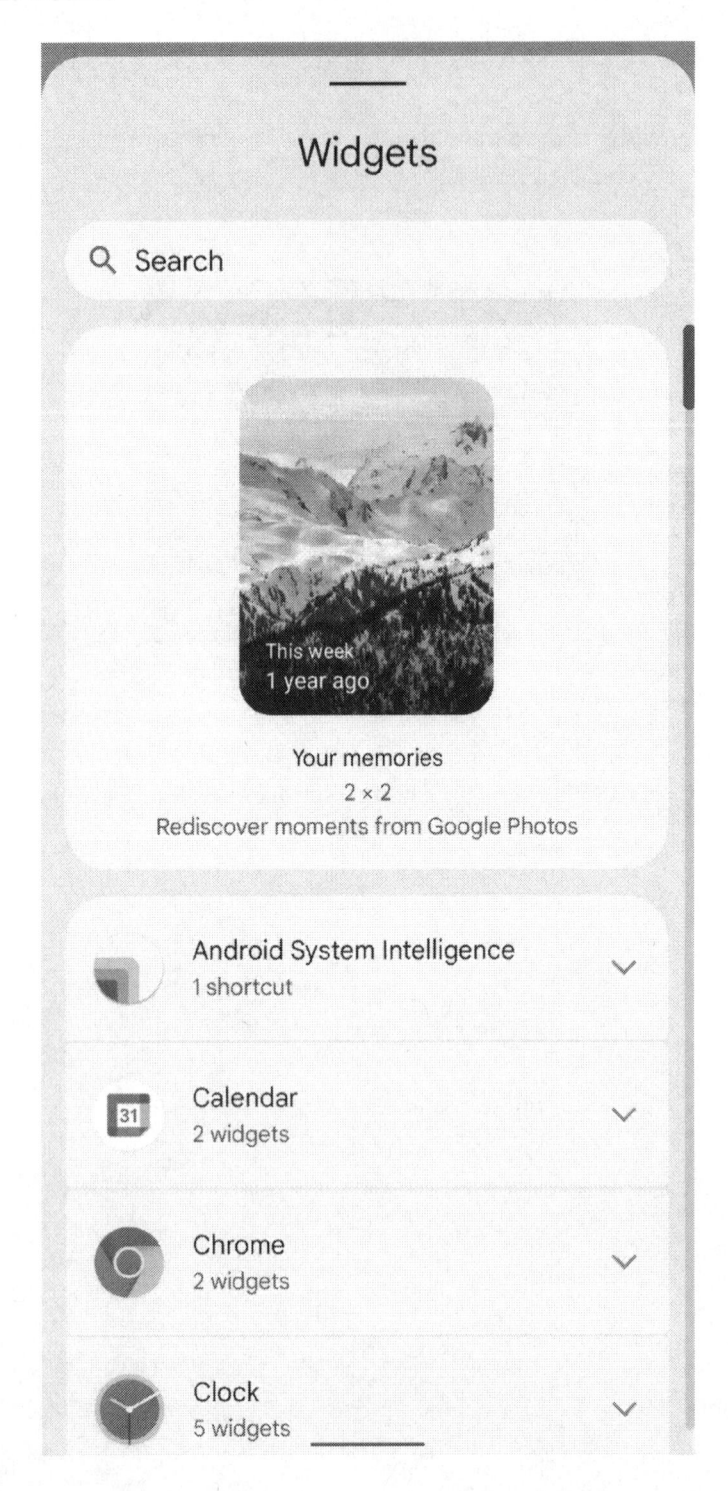

Mastering the Pixel 9 and Pixel 9 Pro

When you find one you want to add, tap and hold it, then drag it to the screen you want to add it to.

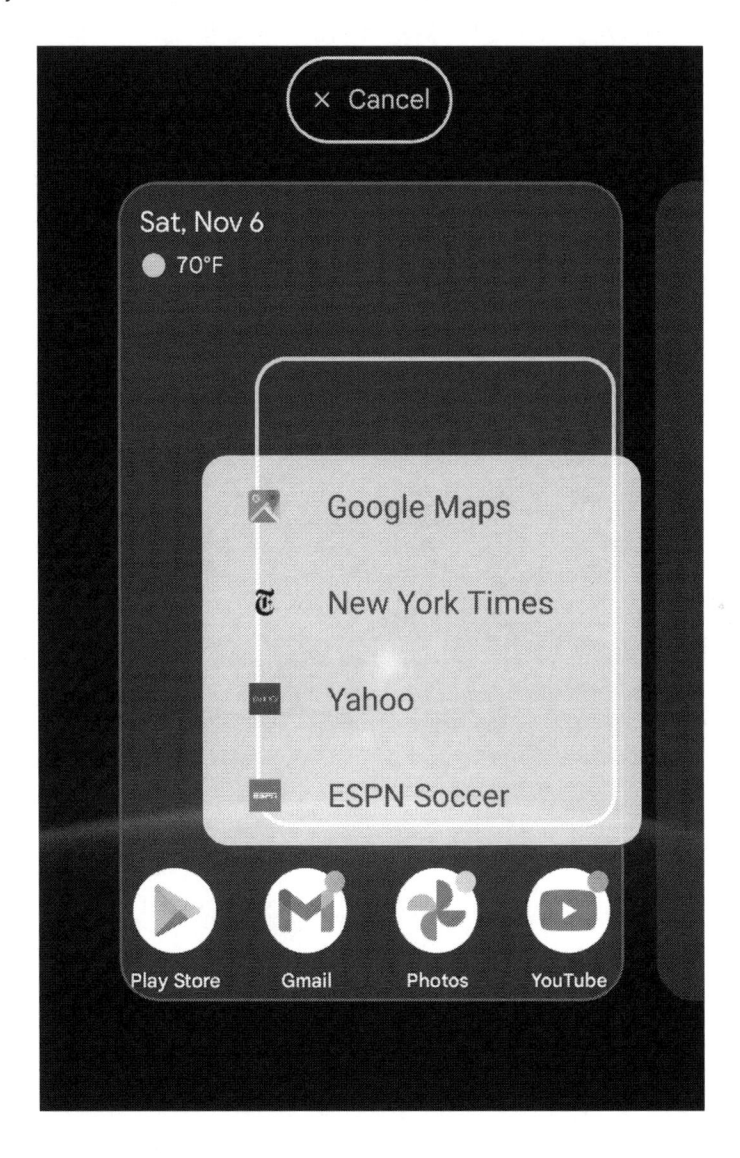

Widgets come in all sorts of shapes and sizes, but most of them can be resized. To resize it, tap and hold it. If you see little circles, then you can tap those and drag it in or out to make it bigger or smaller.

83

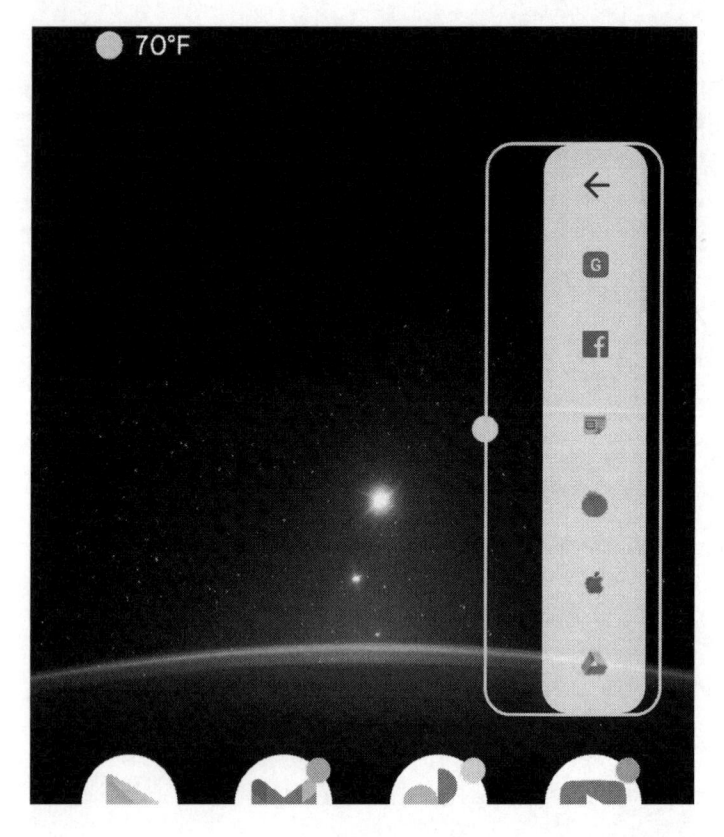

You remove widgets the same way you remove shortcuts. Tap and hold and then drag it upward to the remove.

2:14
Anniversary
Anniversary
Thu, Nov 22
Thanksgiving Day
Tues
Metascrum
7:15 - 8:15 AM
73°F
Fri, Nov 23

Wallpaper

Adding wallpaper to your screen is done in a similar way. Tap and hold your finger on the Home screen, when the menu comes up, select "Wallpaper" instead of "Widgets." Some of the options even move—so the wallpaper always has something moving across your screen—it's like a slow moving movie.

Wallpapers

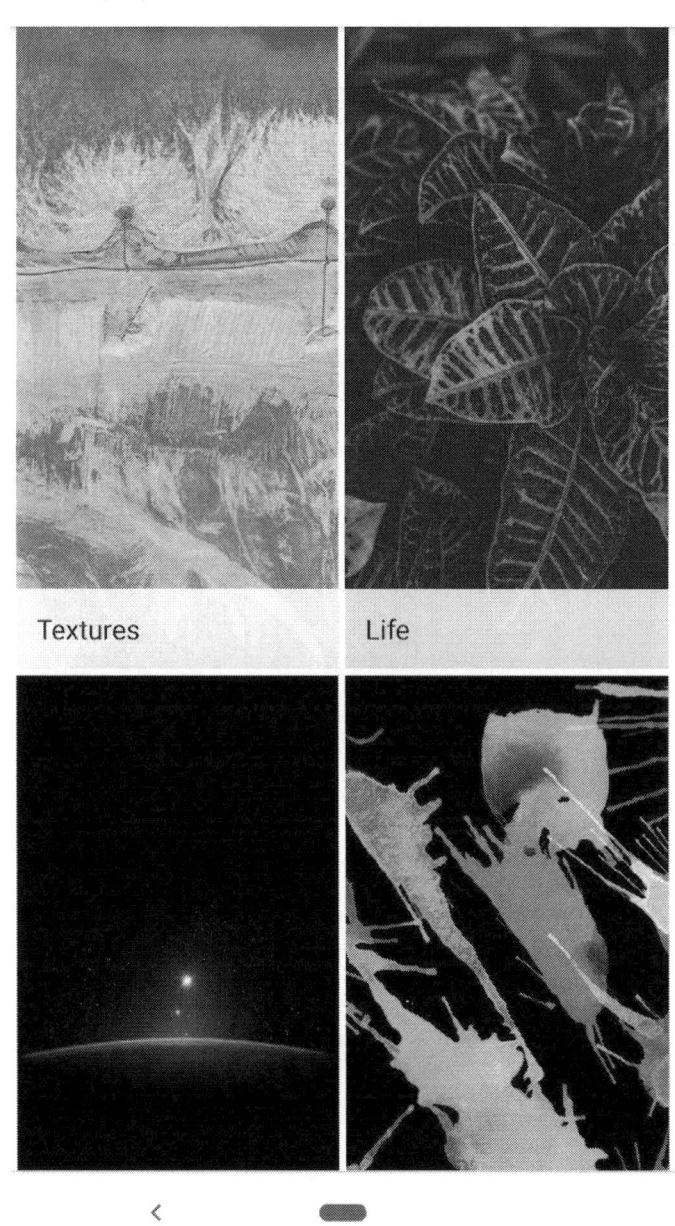

Textures

Life

When you have a wallpaper open that you want to add, just hit the "Set Wallpaper" in the upper right corner.

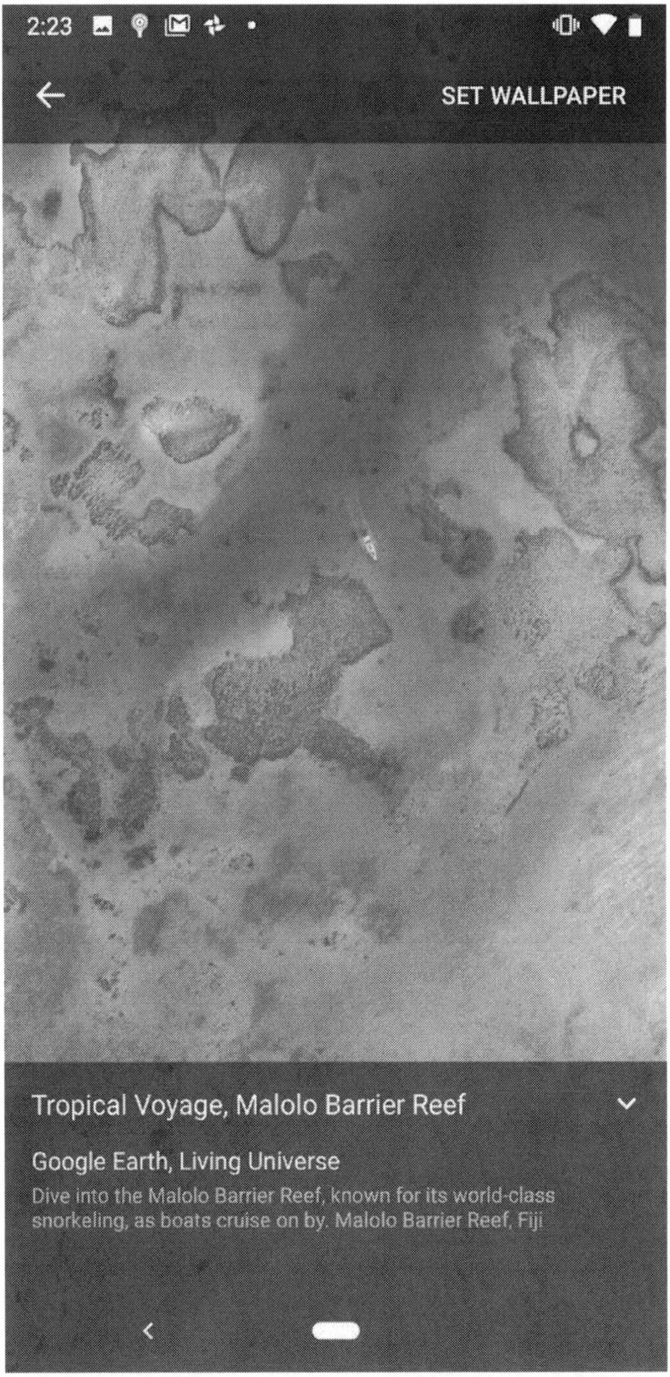
2:23
SET WALLPAPER
Tropical Voyage, Malolo Barrier Reef
Google Earth, Living Universe
Dive into the Malolo Barrier Reef, known for its world-class snorkeling, as boats cruise on by. Malolo Barrier Reef, Fiji

You can also change the style of your phone—such as the colors.

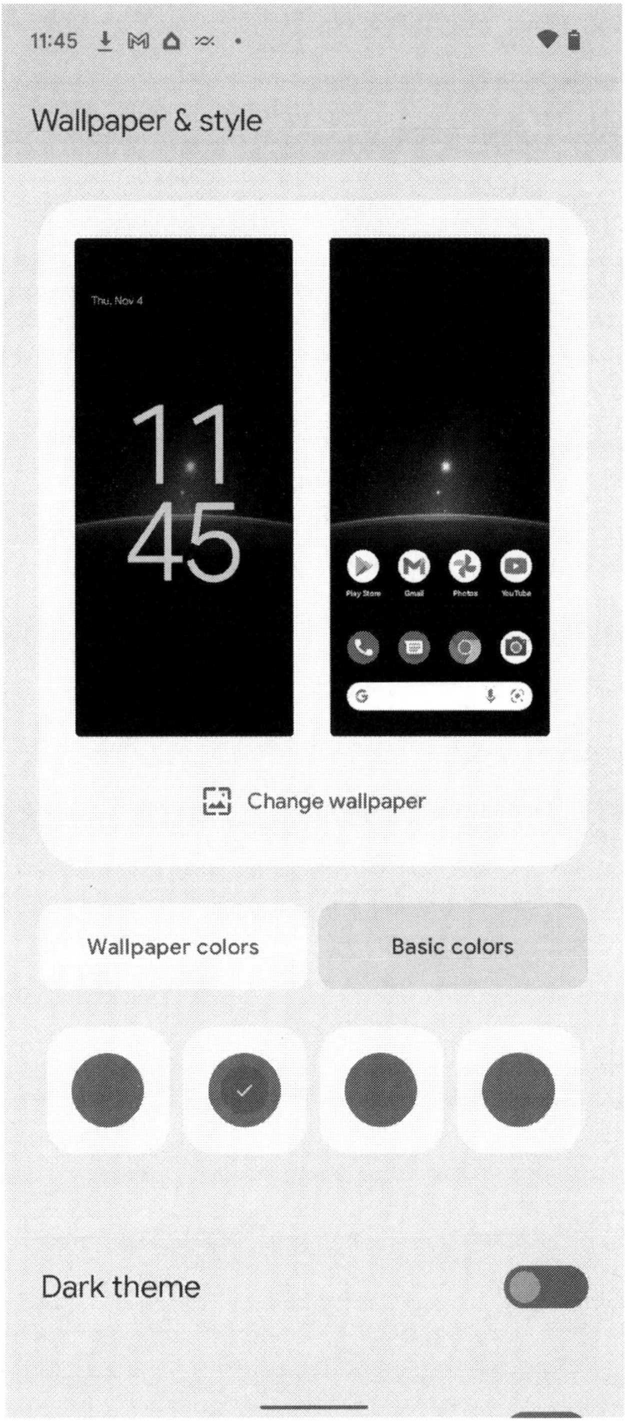
11:45
Wallpaper & style
Thu, Nov 4
11
45
Play Store
Gmail
Photos
YouTube
Change wallpaper
Wallpaper colors
Basic colors
Dark theme

a word, or two, about menus

It's pretty intuitive that if you tap on an icon, it opens the app. What's not so obvious is if you tap and hold there are other options. Every app is different. Usually, they're shortcuts—tapping and holding over the Phone icon, for example, brings up your favorites; doing the same thing over the camera brings up a selfie mode shortcut. Tap and hold over your favorite apps to see what shortcuts are available.

spit screens

The Pixel phone comes in two different sizes; the bigger screen obviously gives you a lot more space, which makes split screen apps a pretty handy feature. It works on the smaller Pixel as well, though it doesn't feel as effective on the smaller screen.

To use this feature, swipe up to bring up multitasking; next, tap the icon above the window you want to turn into split screen (note: this feature is not supported on all apps); if split screen is available, you'll see a menu that has an option for split screen.

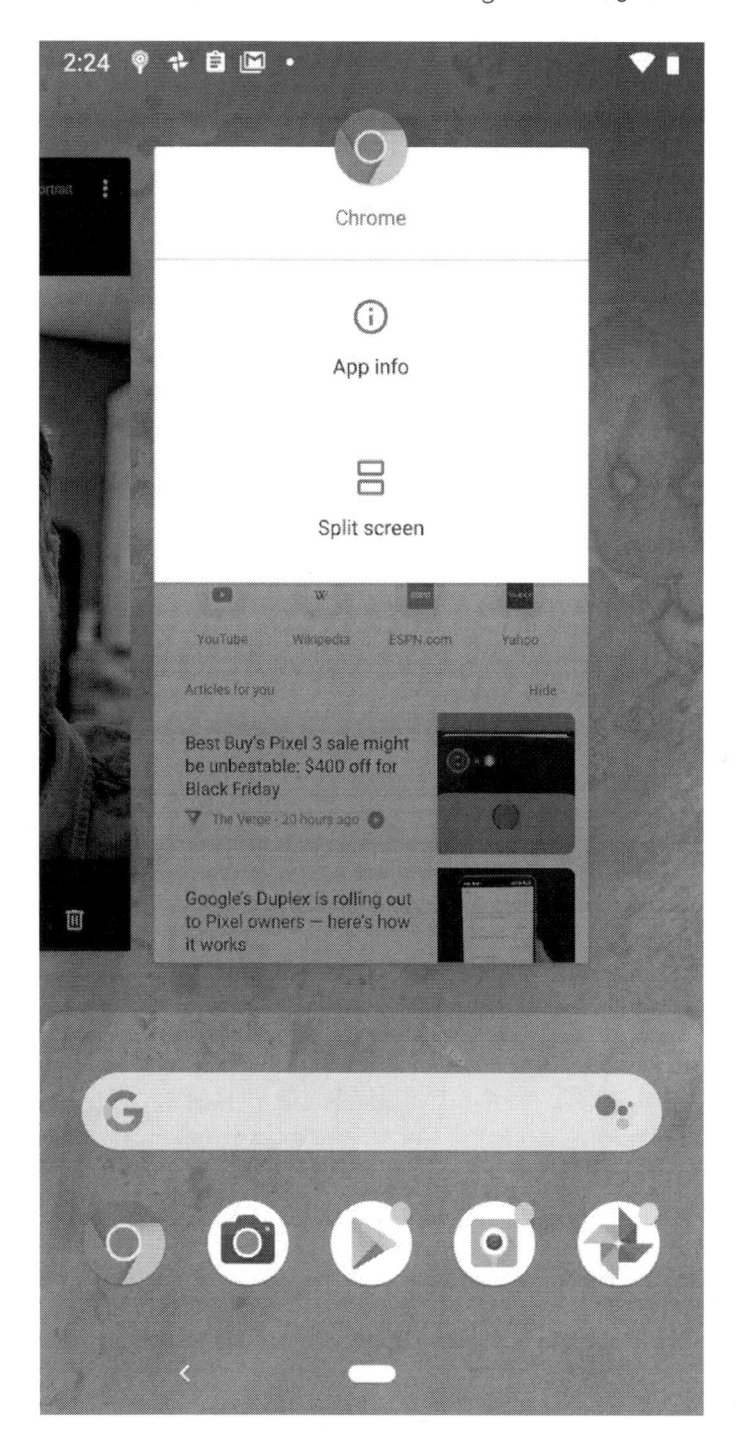

Mastering the Pixel 9 and Pixel 9 Pro

Once you tap "split screen," it will let you swipe left and right to find the app you want to split the screen with. Tap the one you want.

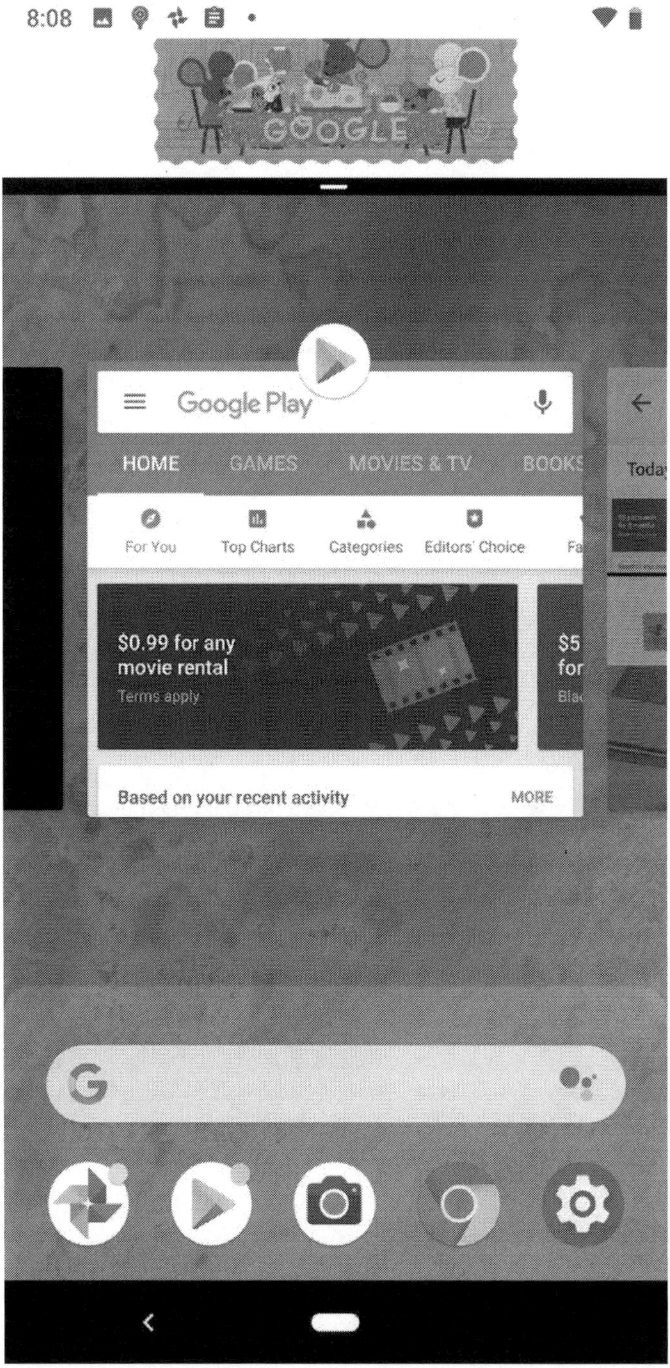
8:08
Google Play
HOME
GAMES
MOVIES & TV
For You
Top Charts
Categories
Editors' Choice
$0.99 for any movie rental
Terms apply
Based on your recent activity
MORE

Your screen is now split in two.

Mastering the Pixel 9 and Pixel 9 Pro

That thin black bar in the middle is adjustable; you can move it up or down so one of the apps has more screen real estate.

To exit this mode, drag the black bar either all the way to the top or all the way to the bottom until one of the apps completely goes away.

gestures

Jump to Camera

Press the power button twice to quickly jump to the camera.

Flip Camera

Switch in and out of selfie mode while you are in the camera by double-twisting the phone.

Double-tap

If your phone is in standby, double-tap the screen and the time and notifications will appear.

Google Assistant

Google Assistant can be trigged by saying "Hey, Google". With gestures, there's a new way: swipe from either the right or left bottom corner.

4 /
the basics...and keep it ridiculously simple

NOW THAT YOU have your phone set up and know your way around the device at its most basic level, let's go over the apps you'll be using the most that are currently on your shortcut or favorite bar:

- Phone
- Messages
- Google Play Store
- Chrome

Notice that Camera is off this list? There's a lot to cover with Camera, so I'll go over it in a separate chapter.

Before we get into it, there's something you need to know: how to open apps not on your favorite bar. It's easy. From your home screen, swipe up from the bottom. Notice that menu that's appearing? That's where all the additional apps are.

Scott La Counte

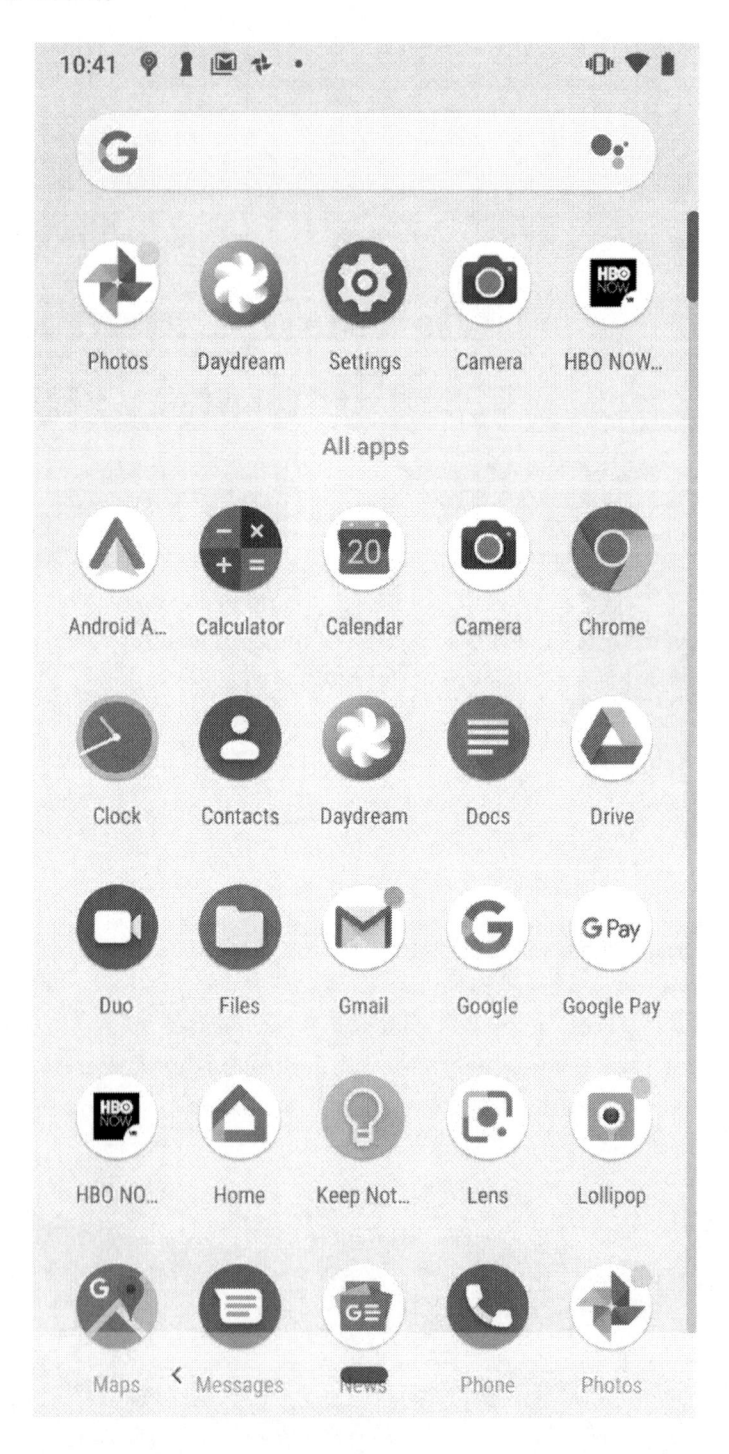

making calls

So...who you going to call? Ghostbusters?!

You would be the most awesome person in the world if Ghostbusters was in your phone contacts! But before you can find that number in your contacts, it would probably help to know how to add a contact, find a contact, edit a contact, and put contacts into groups, right? So before we get to making calls, let's do baby steps and cover Contacts.

Contacts

So, let's open up the Contacts app to get started. See it? Not on your favorite bar, right? So where is it?! That's why I showed you earlier how to get to additional apps. Swipe up from the bottom of your screen and keep swiping until the menu appears in its entirety.

It's in alphabetical order, so the Contacts app is in the C's. It looks like this:

Chances are if you've added your email account, you'll already have a lot of contacts listed. Like hundreds!

You can either scroll slowly, or head to the right-hand side of the app and scroll—this lets you quickly scroll by letters. Just slide your finger until you see the letter of the contact you want and then stop.

Mastering the Pixel 9 and Pixel 9 Pro

I'm getting ahead of myself, however! Before you can scroll, it would be nice to know how to add a contact so there are people to scroll to. To add a contact, tap on that blue plus sign.

Adding a person looks more like applying for a job than adding a contact. There are rows and rows of fields!

   First name

   Last name

   Company

   Phone

   Mobile

   Email

   Home

More fields

Just in case you weren't overwhelmed by all the fields, you can tap more fields and get even more!

Scott La Counte

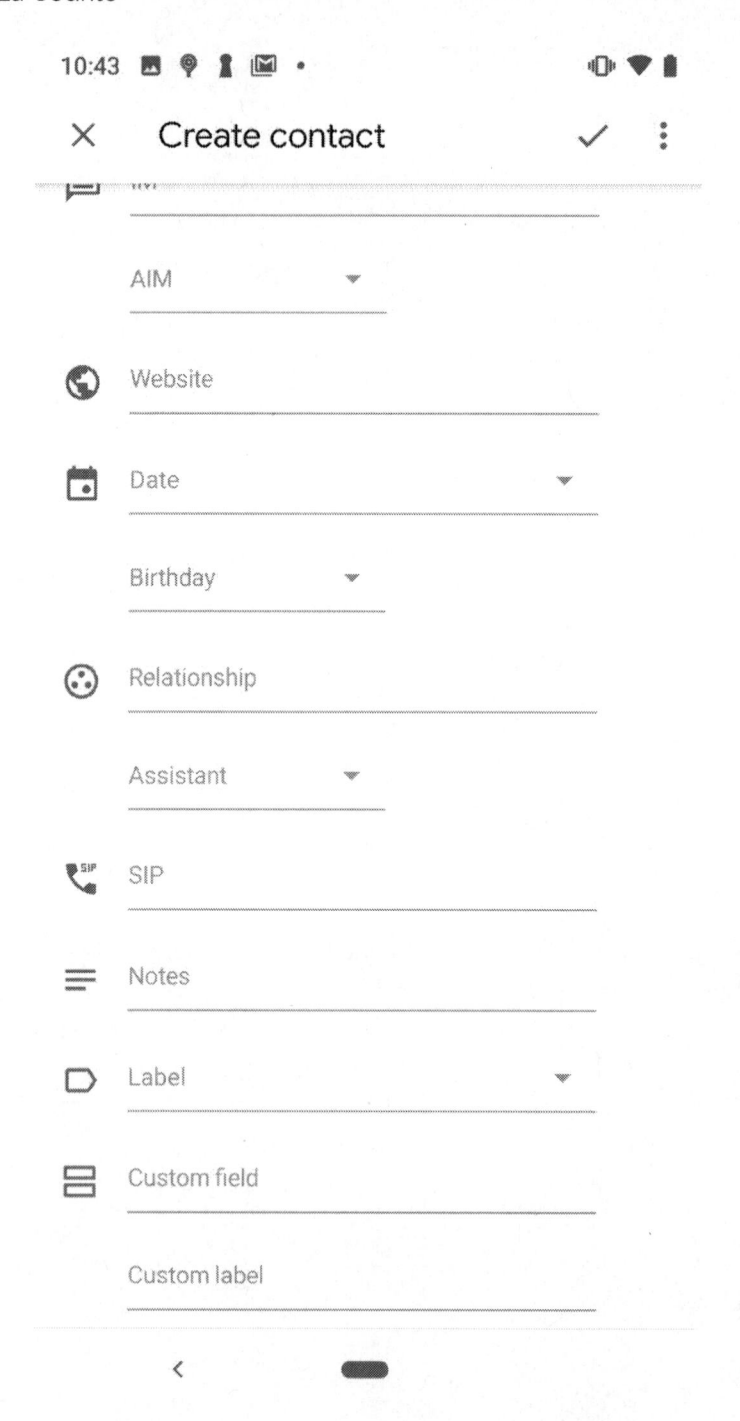

Is that not enough? Google has you covered because you can add a custom field!

Here's the most important thing you need to know: fields are optional! You can add a name and email and that's it. You don't even have to add their phone number. If you want to call them, then that would certainly help though.

If you have a hard time remembering who people are, then you can also take a picture or add a picture you already have. Comes in handy if you have eight kids and you can't remember if Joey is the one with blonde hair or red hair.

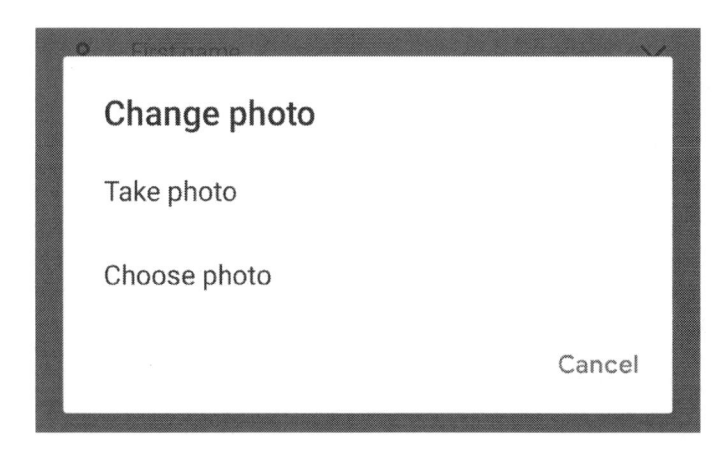

Change photo

Take photo

Choose photo

Cancel

Once you are done, tap the checkbox. That saves it. If you decide you don't want to add a contact after all, the tap the X. That closes it without saving.

Editing a Contact

If you add an email and then later decide you should add a phone number, or if you want to edit anything else, then just find the name in your contacts and tap it once. This brings up all the info you've already added.

107

Go to the lower corner and tap on the pencil button. This makes the contact editable. Go to your desired field and update. When you are finished, tap the checkbox in the upper right corner.

Sharing a Contact

If you have your phone long enough, someone will ask you for so and so's phone number. The old-fashioned way was to write it down. But you have a smartphone, so you aren't old-fashioned!

The new way to share a number is to find the person in your contacts, tap their name, then tap those three dots in the upper right corner of your screen. This brings up a menu.

Delete

Share

Add to Home screen

Set ringtone

Route to voicemail

Help & feedback

There are a few options here, but the one you want is "Share"; from here you have a few options, but the easiest is to text or email the contact to your friend. This sends them a contact card. So if you have other information with that contact (such as email) then that will be sent over as well.

Delete Contact

There are a few more options on that menu I just showed. If you decide a person is dead to you and you never want to contact them again, then you can return to that menu and tap "Delete." This erases them from your phone, but not your life.

Get Organized

Once you start getting lots of contacts, then it's going to make finding someone more time-consuming. Labels helps. You can add a label for "Family" for instance, and then stick all of your family members there.

When you open your contacts and tap those three lines in the upper left corner, you'll see a menu. This is where you'll see your labels. So with labels, you can jump right into that list and find the contact you need.

| Contacts | 393 |

◈ Suggestions ●

Labels

▱ Family

▱ listser

▱ quiet, please

▱ wedding list

▱ YouTube

+ Create label

⚙ Settings

② Help & feedback

Privacy Policy • Terms of Service

You can also send the entire group inside the label an email or text message. So for instance, if your child is turning 2 and you want to remind everyone in your "Family" contact not to come, then just tap on that label, and then tap on the three dots in the upper right corner. This brings up a menu of options.

> Send email
>
> Send message
>
> Remove contacts
>
> Rename label
>
> Delete label

From here, just tap send email or send message.

But what if you don't have labels? Or if you want to add people to a label? Easy. Remember that long application you used to add a contact? One of the fields was called "Labels." You have to tap more to see it. It's all the way at the bottom. One of the last fields, in fact.

≡ Notes

▭ Label ▼

Add custom field

If you've never added a label or want to add a new one, then just start typing. If you have another one that you'd like to use, then just tap the arrow and select it.

When you are done, don't forget to tap "Save."

Delete Label

If you decide you no longer want to have a label, then just go to the menu I showed you above—side menu, then the three dots. From here, tap the "Delete Label."

If there's just one person you want to boot from the label, then tap them and go to the label and delete it.

Making Calls

That concludes our sidetrack into the Contacts app. We can now return to getting back to making phone calls to the Ghostbusters.

You can make a call by opening the Contacts app, then selecting the contact, and then tapping on their phone number. Alternatively, you can tap on the Phone button from your Home screen or favorite bar.

There are a few options when you open this app. Let's talk about each one.

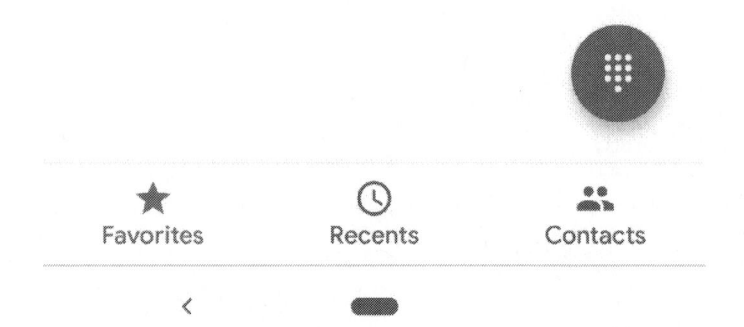

Starting from the far left is the Favorites tab. If you tap this, then you'll see your favorite contacts. If you haven't added any, then this will be empty. If you want to make someone your favorite, then tap them in your Contacts, and tap the star on the top by their name. Once you do that, they'll automatically start showing up here.

In the middle is the Recents tab. If you've made any calls, they'll show here.

The last option is Contacts, which opens a version of the Contacts app that's within the Phone app.

Also on the right is the dial button.

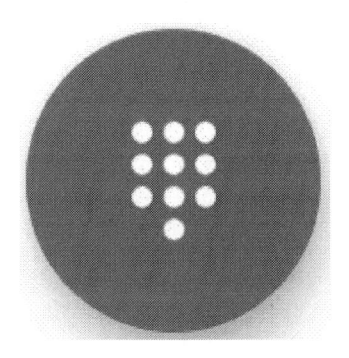

If you want to dial someone the old-fashioned way by tapping in numbers, then tap this.

When you are done with the call, hit the "End" button on your phone.

Answer and Decline Calls

What do you do when someone calls you? Probably ignore it because it's a telemarketer!

It's easy to accept a call, however. When the phone rings, the number will appear and if the person is in your Contacts, then the name will appear as well. To answer, just swipe the "answer." To decline just drag the "decline."

Play Angry Birds While Talking to Angry Mom

What if you're on a call with your mom and she's just complaining about something, but you don't want to be rude and hang up? Easy. You multitask! This means you could play Angry Birds while talking!

To multitask, just swipe up from the bottom of your phone, and open the app you want to work in while you are talking. The call will show in the notification area. Tap it to return to the call.

direct my call

Direct My Call came out in 2021 as a way to help you quickly navigate automated menus. The AI on the Pixel 7 is able to detect the menus and put a call menu on your screen, which makes it easier to get where you want to go before the voice on the line says it. It's a feature that will improve over time, so it may not work as expected at first.

To use it, open the Phone app, then tap the three-dot menu icon in the upper corner and select "Settings." Go to "Direct My Call" then toggle it on.

hold for me

Google Assistant has become quite literally, your assistant. This is especially true on phone calls. Have you ever been on hold for way too long? Google Assistant knows your pain and is willing to hold for you! It will tell you when it detects a human has picked up. To use it, open the Phone app, tap the three-dot menu in the upper-right corner and select "Settings." Last, tap "Hold for Me."

don't be spammy

Nobody likes that call asking if you want to buy something. Google can help filter your calls and get rid of spam. To turn it on go to the Phone app, then tap those three dots in the upper right corner, and tap settings. Go to "Spam and Call Screen." Tap the toggle next to "See caller and spam ID".

messages

Now that you know how Contacts and Phone works, messaging will be like second nature. They share many of the same properties.

Let's open up the Messages app (it's on your Favorites bar).

Create / Send a Message

When you have selected the contact(s) to send a message to, tap Compose. You can also manually type in the number in the text field.

You can add more than one contact--this is known as a group text.

Use the text field to type out your message. If you want to add anything fancy to your message (like photos or gifs) then tap the plus sign. This brings up a menu with more options.

Scott La Counte

When you are ready to send your message, tap the arrow with the SMS under it.

View Message

When you get a message, your phone will vibrate, chirp, or do nothing—it all depends on how you set up your phone. To view the message, you can either open the app, or swipe down to see your notifications—one will be the text message.

Conversations

Google took big strides in Android 11 to make replying to messages more streamlined and effortless.

One place you see this is with Conversations. When you get a message (text, Facebook message, Twitter message, etc), you'll see that in your notification area by swiping down from the top.

The old method was to click that message to reply. Now you can see the message, set the priority level, and reply right from this area.

Chat Bubbles

Another area you'll see Android streamline approach to messages is with Chat Bubbles. Chat Bubbles will appear on the side of whatever app you are working in, so you can reply without actually closing the app. As the name suggests, they'll be little bubbles on the side of your screen.

If you aren't crazy about this feature, you can toggle it off by going to the Settings app, then Apps & Notifications> Notifications > Bubbles.

Scott La Counte

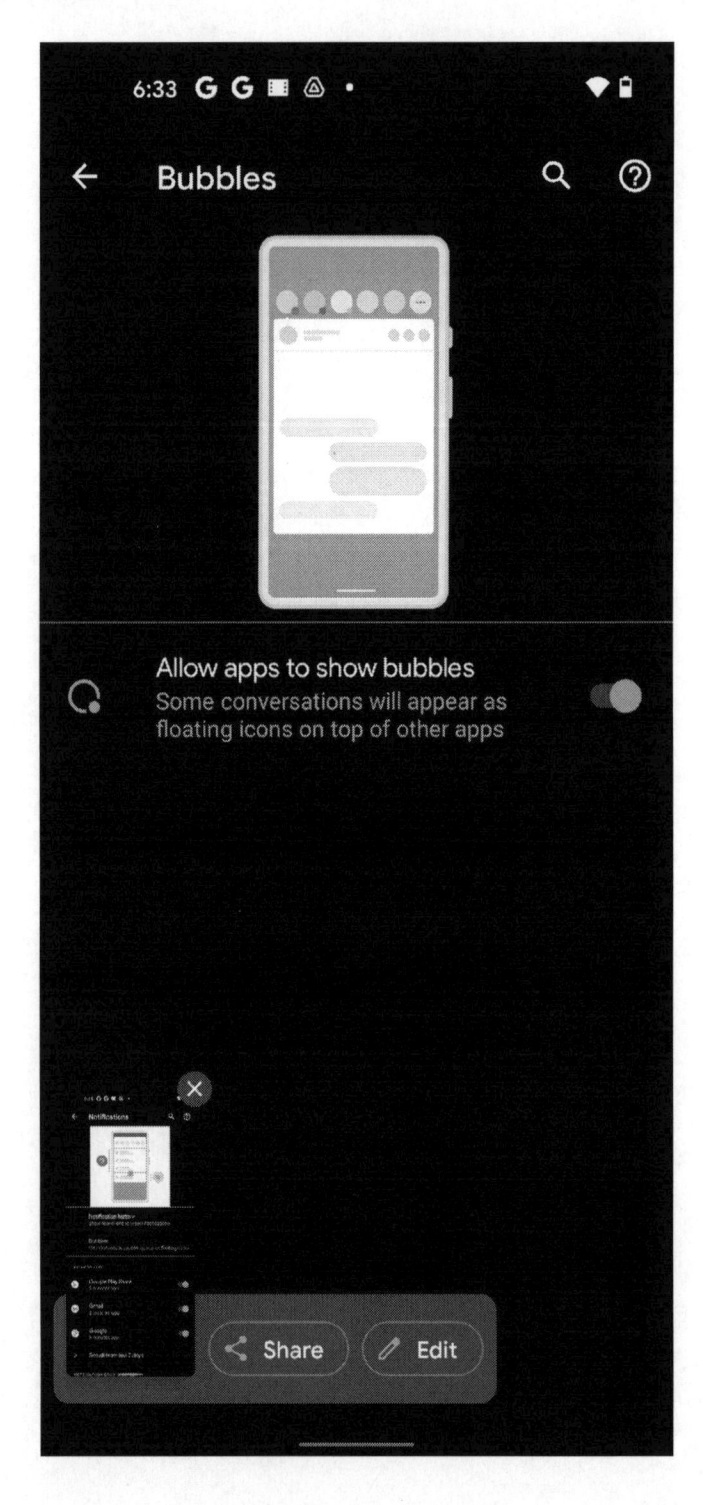

Smart Reply

If you're a Gmail user, you've probably started to see Smart Replies in your email. Smart Reply uses a computer engine to recognize what you will type next and make a suggestion.

Smart Reply works so surprisingly well you might be a little creeped out by it—like it will feel like some person is on the other end of the screen reading your messages! That's not the case. It's all artificial intelligence. But if you still find the feature either creepy or annoying then you can go to the Settings app, then search for Smart Reply. Under Suggestions in chat, you'll see a on / off toggle for the feature.

Suggestions in chat

Assistant suggestions

EXAMPLE
- Movies near me

Smart Reply

EXAMPLE
- Thank you

Suggested actions

EXAMPLE
- Share location

Suggested stickers
Show suggested stickers

Smart Reply, suggested actions, and Assistant suggestions are generated with on-device intelligence by Messages.

Suggestions are not shared with Google or anyone else until you tap them.

If you allow Messages to access your device's location, you'll see more local suggestions. Learn more

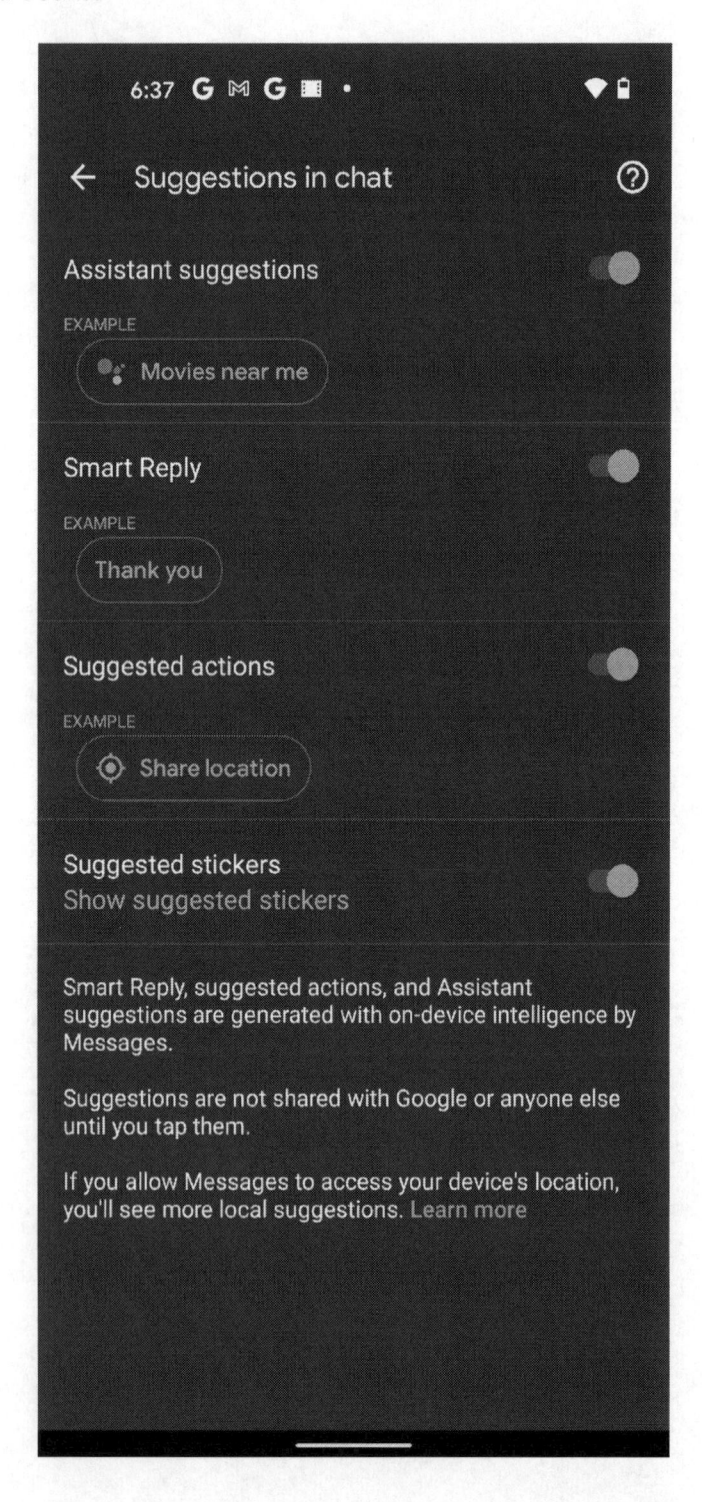

where's an app for that?

I mentioned earlier that you could play Angry Birds while talking to your angry mom on the phone. Sound fun? But where is Angry Birds on your phone? It's not! You have to download it.

Adding and removing apps on the Pixel is easy. Head to your favorite bar on the bottom of your Home screen and tap the Google Play app.

This launches the Play Store.

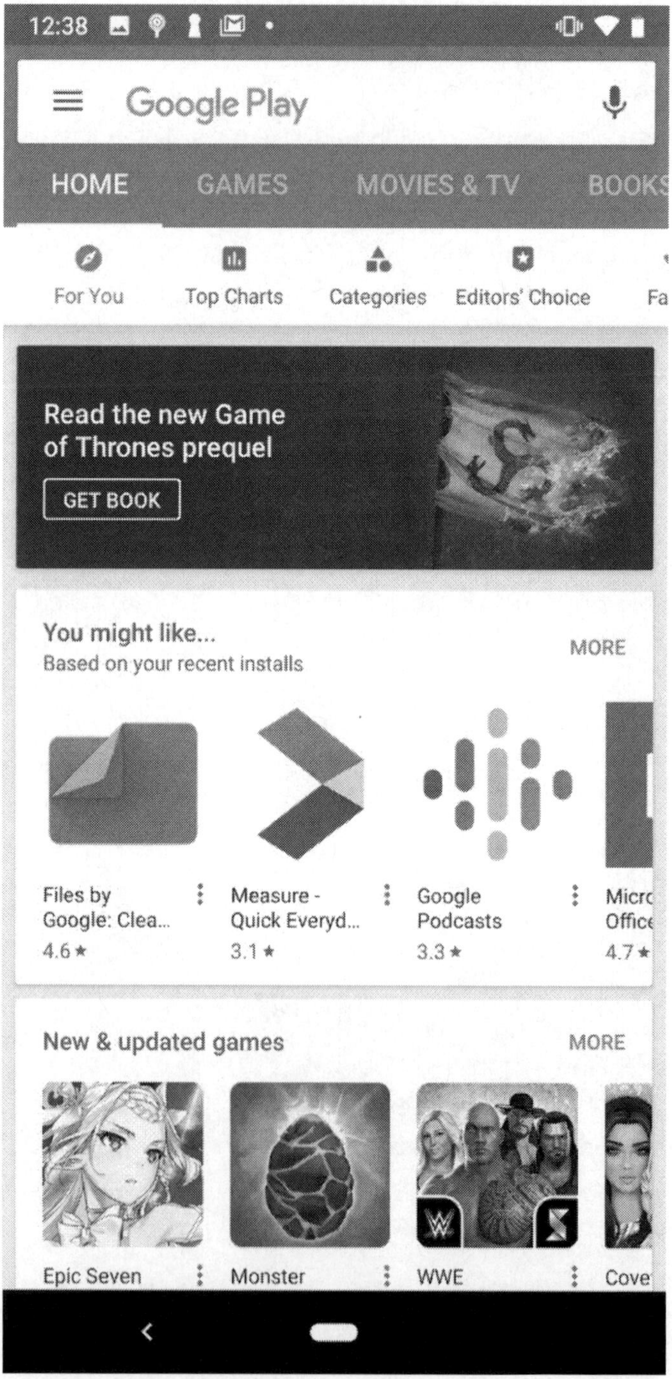
12:38
Google Play
HOME
GAMES
MOVIES & TV
For You
Top Charts
Categories
Editors' Choice
Read the new Game of Thrones prequel
GET BOOK
You might like...
Based on your recent installs
MORE
Files by Google: Clea...
4.6
Measure - Quick Everyd...
3.1
Google Podcasts
3.3
New & updated games
MORE
Epic Seven
Monster
WWE

From here you can browse the top apps, see editors' picks, look through categories, or, if you have an app in mind, search for it. The Play Store isn't just for apps. You can use the tabs on the top to go to movies, books, and music. Any kind of downloadable content that's offered by Google can be found here.

When you see the app you want, tap on it. You can read through reviews, see screenshots, and install it on your phone. To install, simply tap the install button—if it's a paid app you'll be prompted to buy it. If there's no price, it's free (or offers in-app payments—which means the app is free, but there are premium features inside it you may have to pay for).

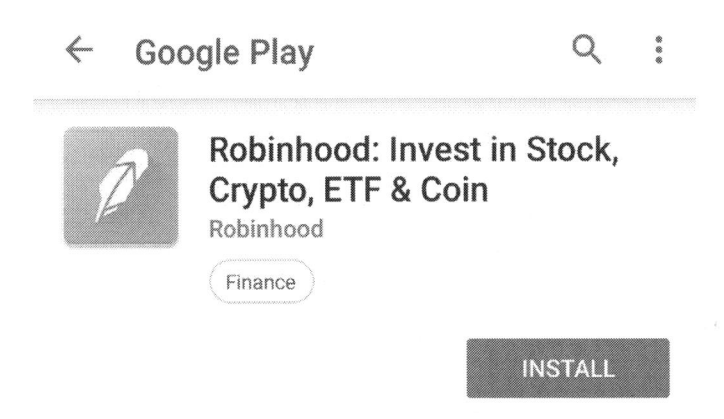

The app is now stored in the app section of your device (remember the section you get to when you swipe up from the bottom to the top?).

Remove App

If you decide you no longer want an app, go to the app in the app menu and tap and hold it. This brings up a box that says "App info." Tap that.

Scott La Counte

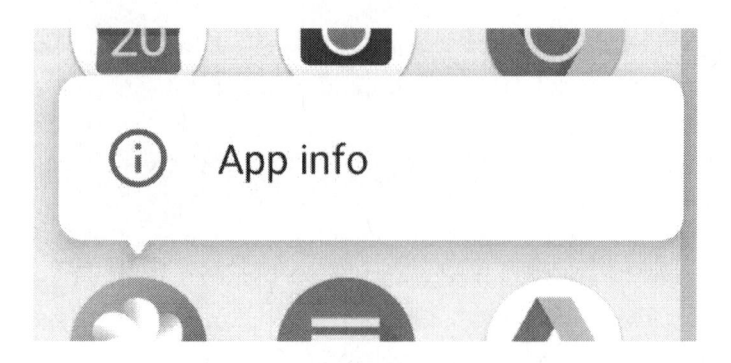

From this menu, you'll get all the information about the app; one of the options is to remove it. Tap that and you're done.

Notifications
On

Permissions
No permissions granted

Storage
153 MB used in internal storage

Data usage
82.75 MB used since Oct 25

Advanced
Time spent in app, Battery, Open by default, Sto..

If you download the app from the Play Store, you can always delete it. Some apps that were pre-installed on your phone cannot be deleted.

driving directions

Back in the day, you may have had a GPS. It was a fancy plastic device that would give you directions for anywhere in North America. You can throw out that device because your phone is your new GPS.

To get directions, swipe up to open up your apps. Tap the Maps app.

It's automatically going to be set to wherever you are currently at—which is both creepy and useful.

To get started, just type where you want to go. I'm searching for an amusement park in Anaheim.

Mastering the Pixel 9 and Pixel 9 Pro

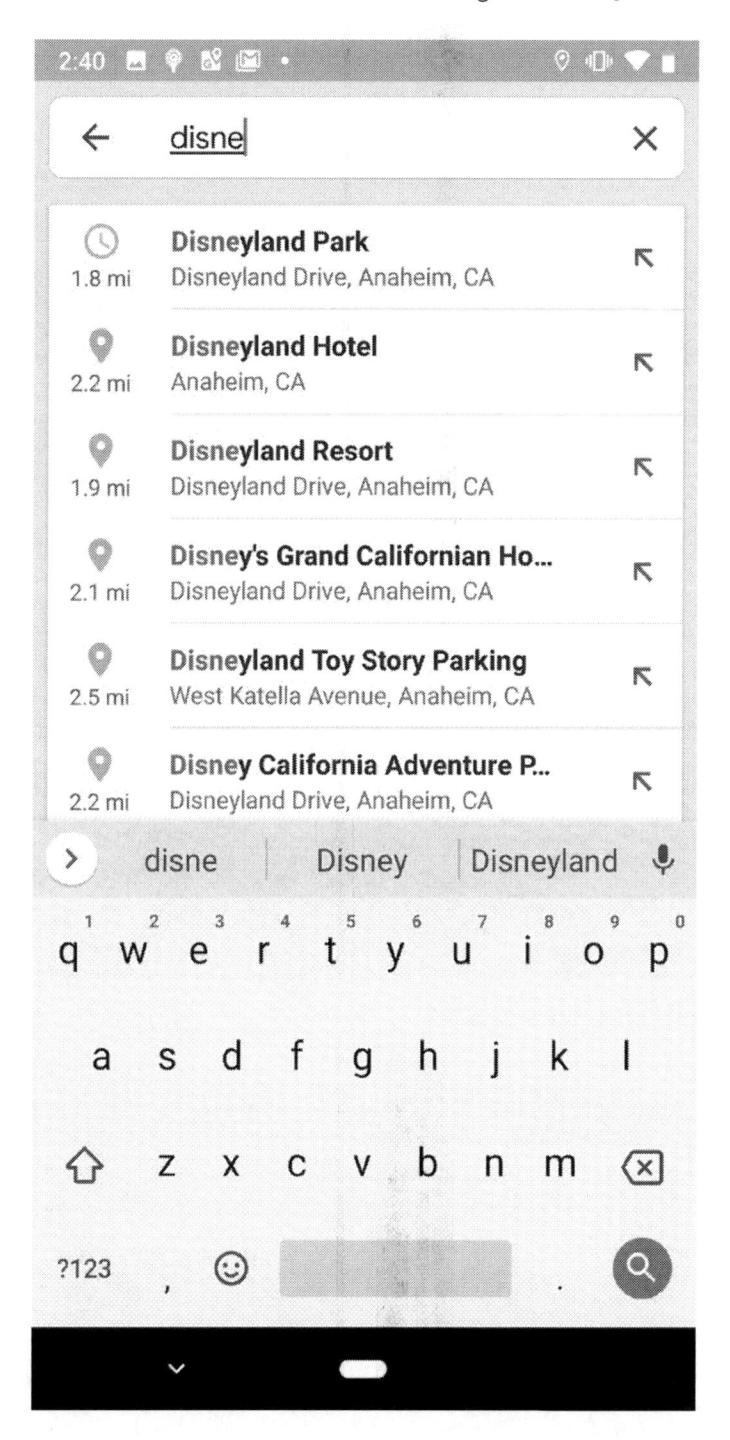

It automatically starts filling in what it thinks you are going to type and tells you the distance. When you see the one you want, tap it.

It pinpoints the location on the map and also gives you an option to call, share or get directions to the location. If you want to zoom out or in, just use two fingers and pinch in or out on the screen.

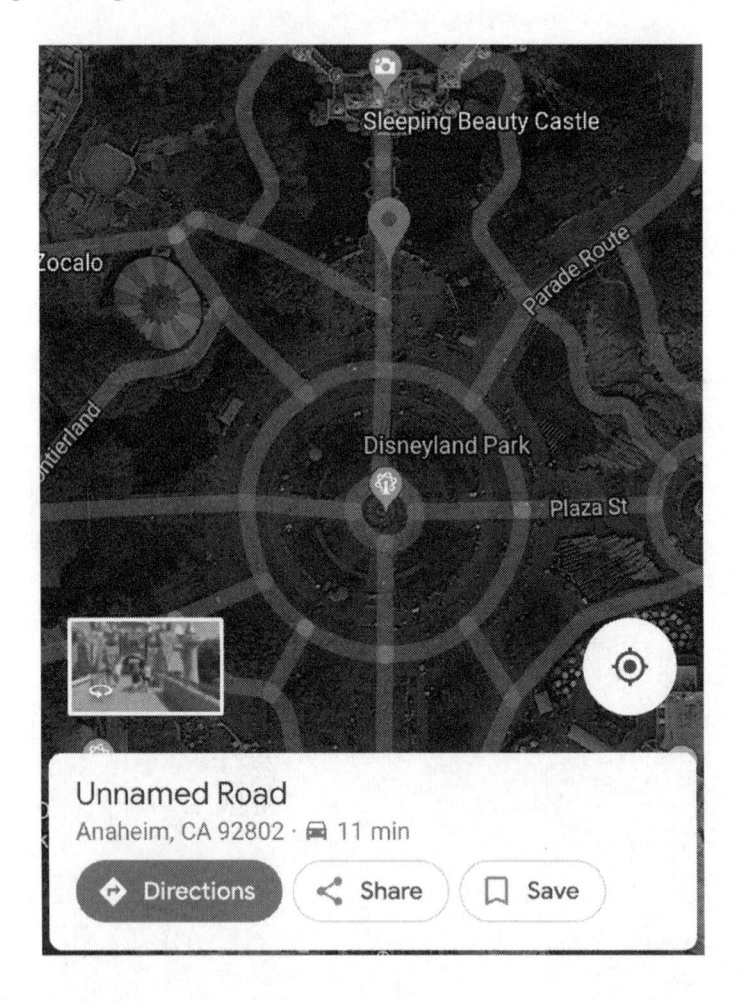

It automatically gets directions from where you are. Want it from a different location? Just tap on the "Your location" field and type where you want to go. You can also reverse the directions by tapping on the double arrows. When you are ready to go, tap "Start."

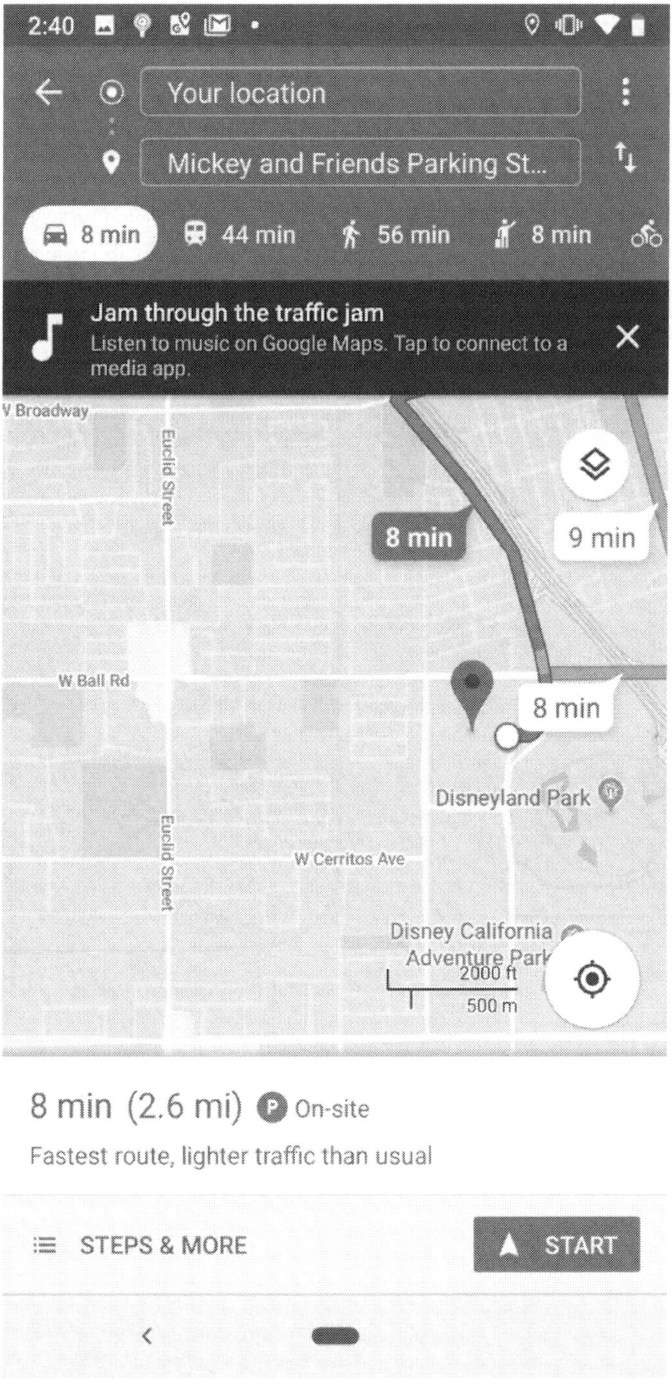
2:40
Your location
Mickey and Friends Parking St...
8 min
44 min
56 min
8 min
Jam through the traffic jam
Listen to music on Google Maps. Tap to connect to a media app.
V Broadway
Euclid Street
8 min
9 min
W Ball Rd
8 min
Disneyland Park
W Cerritos Ave
Euclid Street
Disney California Adventure Park
2000 ft
500 m
8 min (2.6 mi)
On-site
Fastest route, lighter traffic than usual
STEPS & MORE
START

What if you don't want to drive? What if you want to walk? Or bike? Or take a taxi? There are options for all of those and more! Tap the slider under the address bar to whatever you prefer. This updates the directions—when you walk, for example, it will show you one-way streets and also update the time it will take you.

What if you want to drive but are like me: terrified of freeways in California? There's an option to avoid highways. Tap the menu button in the upper right corner of the screen, then select what you want to avoid, and hit "done." You are now rerouted to a longer route—notice how the times probably changed?

Options

☐ Avoid highways

☐ Avoid tolls

☐ Avoid ferries

CANCEL   DONE

Once you get your directions, you can swipe up to get turn-by-turn directions. You can even see what it looks like from the street. It's called Street View.

8 min (2.6 mi)

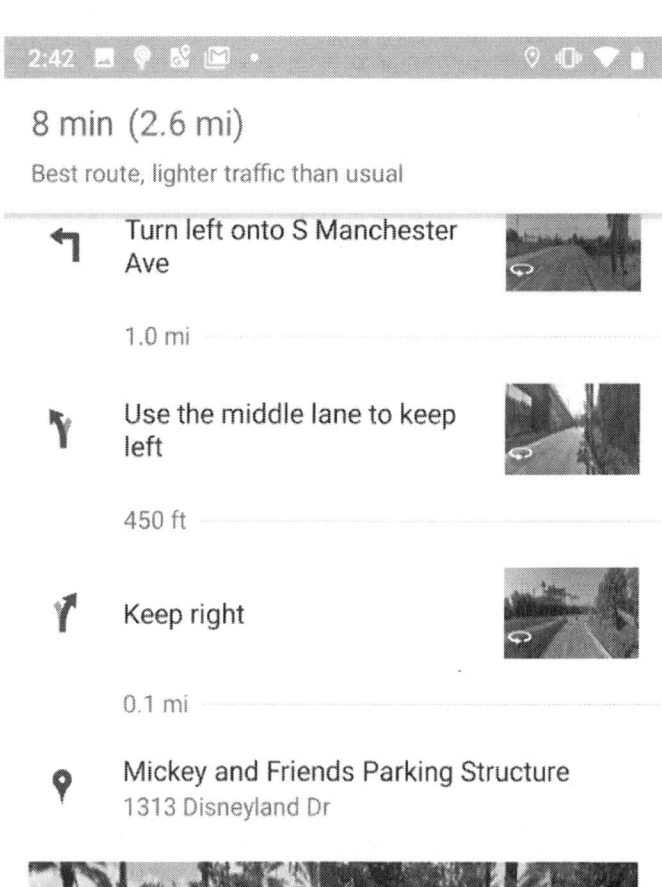

Best route, lighter traffic than usual

↰ Turn left onto S Manchester Ave

1.0 mi

Use the middle lane to keep left

450 ft

Keep right

0.1 mi

📍 **Mickey and Friends Parking Structure**
1313 Disneyland Dr

SHOW MAP   START

Street View isn't only for streets. Google is expanding the feature everywhere. If you hold your finger over the map, there will be an option to show Street View if it's available. Just tap the thumbnail. Here's a Street View:

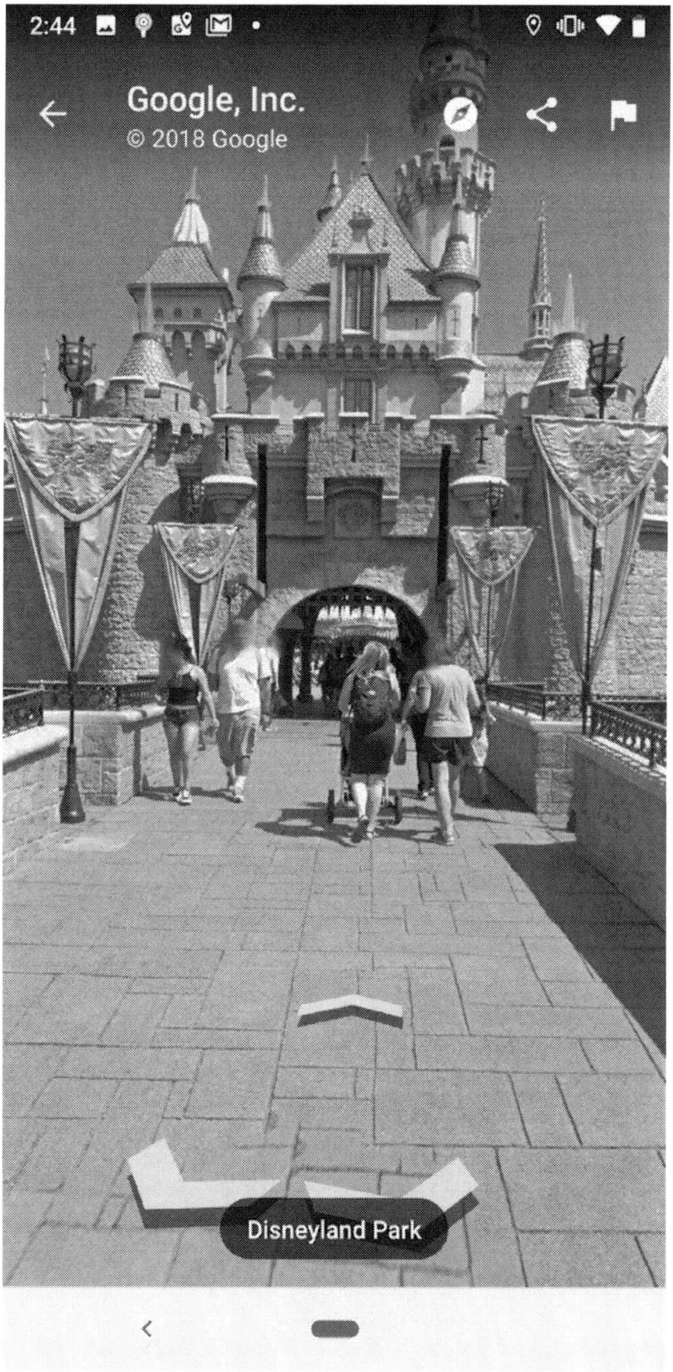
2:44
Google, Inc.
© 2018 Google
Disneyland Park

You can wander around the entire park! If only you could ride the rides, too! You can get even closer to the action by picking up the Dreamview headset. When you stick your phone in that, you can turn your head and the view turns with you.

Street View is also available in a lot of malls and other tourist attractions. Point your map to the Smithsonian in Washington, DC and get a pretty cool Street View.

what's the name of that song?

We've all had that moment where we are sitting in a coffee shop or standing in an elevator and that "one" song plays. The one we love or hate or just want to know the name to. Yes, there's an app to tell us the name, but sometimes we can't pull it out in time—or we just don't want yet another app on our phone. That's where Now Playing comes in handy.

Now Playing has been around since the Pixel 2, but it often goes unnoticed. It detects music playing around you and adds them to a list that you can look at later. It's all in the background and you don't even know it's running unless you've set up notifications.

To see the songs that have been recorded in your log, go to Settings > Sound > Now Playing. You can see your log by clicking on the history, or you can toggle on the "show songs on lock screen" button.

← Now Playing

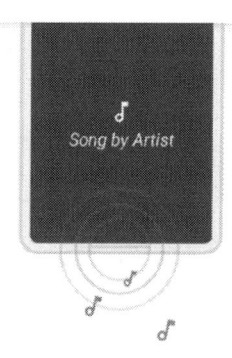

♪ Show songs on lock screen

Now Playing History
Let It Go (From "Frozen"/Soundtrack Version) by Idina Menzel • 21 seconds ago

Now Playing never sends audio or background conversations to Google.

Now Playing protects your privacy using on-device recognition and privacy preserving analytics. Learn more.

live captioning

One of the bigger features to Android 10 is live captioning; live captioning can transcribe any video you record and show what's being said. It works surprisingly well and is pretty accurate.

To turn it on, go to Settings > Sound > Live Caption.

7:44   ← Live Caption

Live Caption

Settings

Language
English only. More languages coming soon.

Hide profanity
Profanity will be replaced with an asterisk symbol *

Show sound labels
Includes sounds like laughter, applause and music *

Live Caption in volume control

ⓘ Live Caption detects speech in media and automatically generates captions.

When showing captions, this feature uses

In the settings, you can also toggle off profanity, and, coming soon, select a different language. If it's something you'd only occasionally use, I recommend leaving it toggled off, but having it toggle on under Live Caption in volume control. With that toggled on, all you have to do is press the volume button. Once you do that, you'll see the option to turn it on; it's the bottom option.

Once it's on, you'll start seeing a transcription appear in seconds.

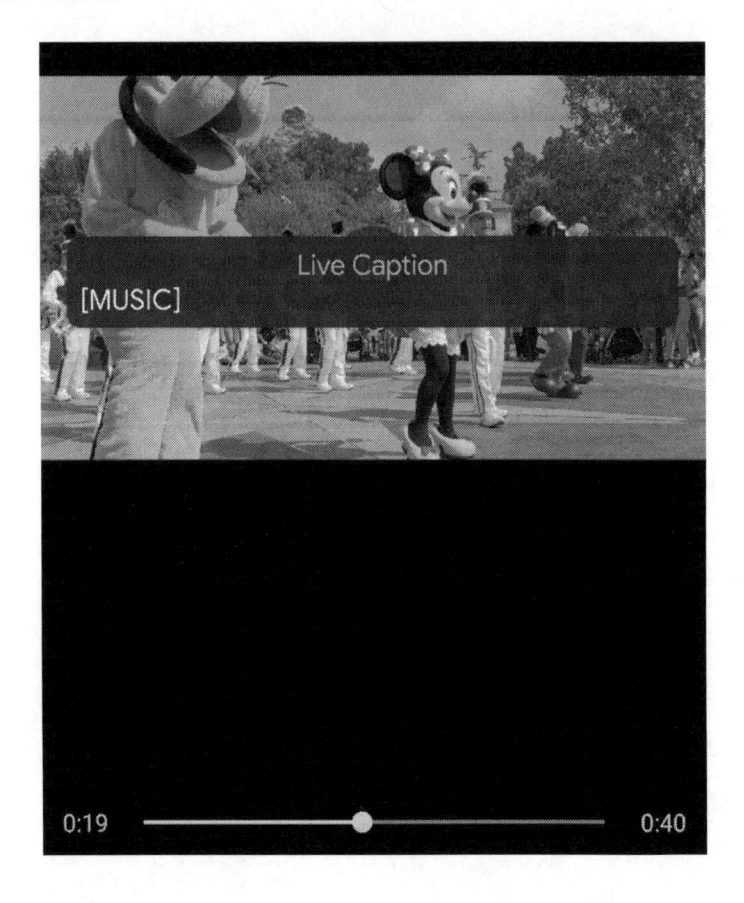

refresh rate

The Pixel 5 supports up to 90Hz refresh rate. Wow, right? Actually, most people have no idea what this means. It's frames per second (FPS)—or 90 FPS. So, what does that mean? If you're playing games or using something that has fast moving action, it means things will seem a lot smoother. It will also eat your battery life to shreds, so use with caution (60Hz is the norm).

To toggle it on / off there are two options. The first way is to go to Settings > Display > Advanced > Smooth Display. This is going to turn it on / off automatically.

If you want to force it on, then there's a second option. Note: this option is "use at your own risk" because it's a developer option. My advice is not to use it unless you know what you are doing. To do it, go to Settings > About phone; go to the very bottom and tap the Build number several times until you are in developer mode. Now go to System > Advanced > Developer Options > Force 90Hz refresh rate.

sharing wi-fi

Anytime you have guests over, you almost always get the question: what's your wi-fi password. If you are like me, then it probably annoys you. Maybe your password is really long, maybe you just don't like giving out your password, or maybe you are just too embarrassed to say that it's "Feet$Fetish-Lover1." Whatever the reason, then you will love sharing your wi-fi with QR codes. Gone are the days of giving this info out. Just give them a code that they scan, and they'll have access without ever knowing what your password is.

To use it, go to your wi-fi settings, then select the configure button for the wi-fi you want to share.

This will bring up your wi-fI info; tap the blue "Share" option with the QR code.

Jeremiah 27:11
Connected

Forget   Share

Signal strength
Good

Frequency
2.4 GHz

Security
WPA2-Personal

Advanced
Network usage, Privacy, Add device, Network d..

Once you verify that it's you, then you will see the code to scan and you just have to show it to your friend.

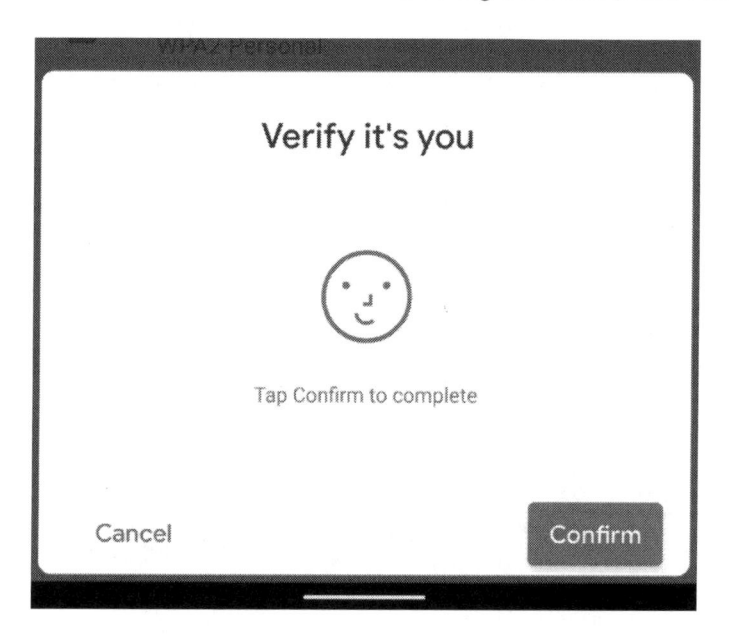

screenshot

If you've ever run into a problem with your phone and they said, "Take a Screenshot of it" then what they mean on Android is to hold your power button and volume down at the same time. That will screenshot whatever is on your screen and put it in a folder in your photos. Just click library when you open your photo album and you'll see a folder called screenshots.

When you do power + volume down, you'll see a preview appear in your lower left corner. It will disappear in a few seconds, unless you tap that you want to edit it.

If the screen allows it (not all will, so don't get frustrated if you don't see this option at first), you can capture more than what's on your screen; it's called a scrolling screenshot. If available, then you'll see a button that says Capture More. This kind of capture is great for long, text heavy, webpages.

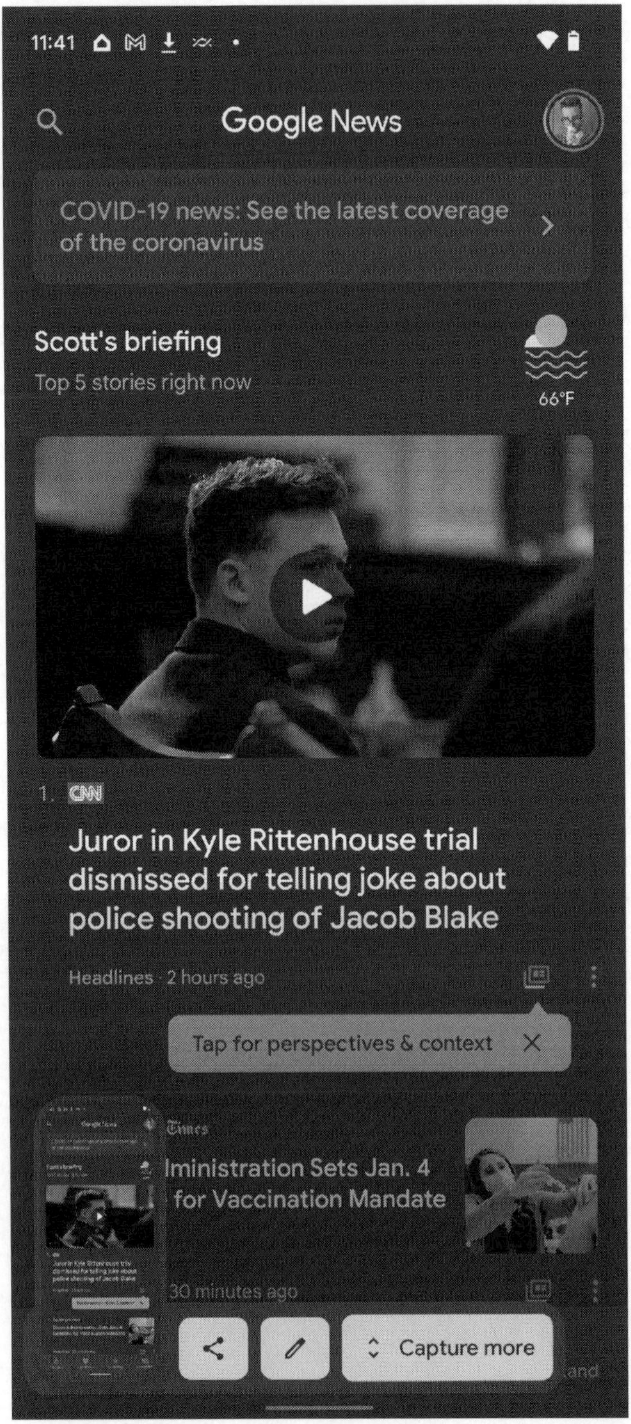
11:41
Google News
COVID-19 news: See the latest coverage of the coronavirus
Scott's briefing
Top 5 stories right now
66°F
1.
Juror in Kyle Rittenhouse trial dismissed for telling joke about police shooting of Jacob Blake
Headlines · 2 hours ago
Tap for perspectives & context
lministration Sets Jan. 4
for Vaccination Mandate
30 minutes ago
Capture more

When you tap Capture more, you'll be given the option to drag over the area you want to capture more of. You can do the entire page or just part of it.

Scott La Counte

google recorder

Google Recorder has always been a student dream by transcribing what is being recorded automatically. It gets better with the Pixel 7 (though the feature was not available at this writing) by letting you label who's speaking; if, for example, you have an interview with several people, it will detect who is saying what.

Scott La Counte

5 /
let's go surfing now!

WHEN IT COMES to the Internet, there are two things you'll want to do:

- Send email
- Browse the Internet

add an email account

When you set up your phone, you'll set it up to your Google Account, which is usually your email.

You may, however, want to add another email account—or remove the one you set up.

To add an email, swipe up to bring up your apps, and tap on "Settings."

Next, tap on "Accounts."

From here, select "Add Account"; you can also tap on the account that's been set up and tap remove account—but remember you can have more than one account on your phone.

Once you add your email, you'll be asked what type of email it is. Follow the steps after you select the email type to add in your email, password, and other required fields.

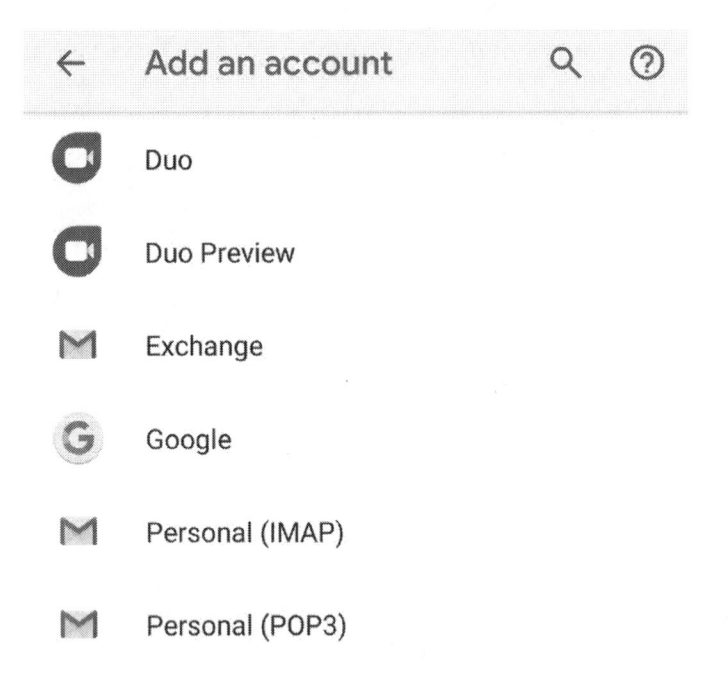

	Add an account	
	Duo	
	Duo Preview	
	Exchange	
	Google	
	Personal (IMAP)	
	Personal (POP3)	

create and send an email

To send an email using Gmail (Pixel's native email app), swipe up to get to your apps, tap "Gmail," and tap "Compose a New Email" (the little round red pencil in the lower right corner). When you're done, tap the send button.

You can also use the Google Play Store to find other email apps (such as Outlook).

manage multiple email accounts

If you have more than one Gmail account, tap the three lines at the upper left of your email screen; this brings out a slider menu. If you tap on the little arrow next to the email address, it drops down and will show other accounts. If none are listed, you can add one.

surfing the internet

Google's native Web browser is Chrome. You can use other browsers (which can be found in the Google Play Store). This book will only cover Chrome, however.

Get started by tapping on the Chrome browser icon from your favorite bar, or by going into all programs.

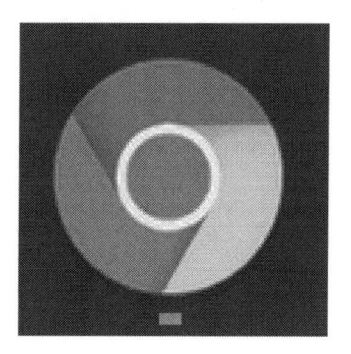

If you've used Chrome on a desktop or any other device, then this chapter won't exactly be rocket science—just like the email app, many of the same properties you find on the desktop exist on the mobile version.

When you open it, you'll see it's a pretty basic browser. There are three main things that you'll want to note.

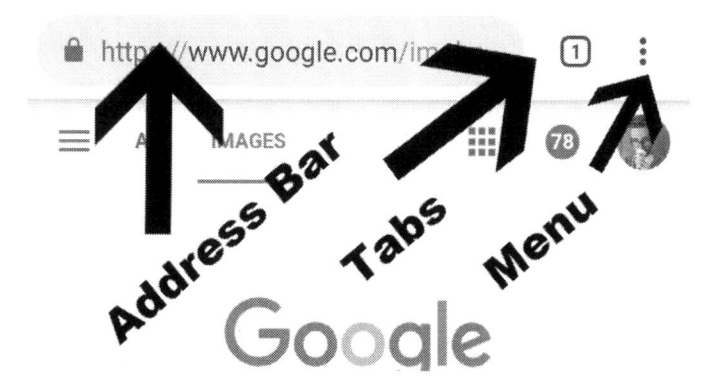

- **Address Bar** - As you would guess, this is where you put the Internet address you want to go to (google.com, for example);

what you should understand, however is that this is not just an address bar. This is a search bar. You can use it to search for things just as you would searching for something on Google; when you hit the enter key, it takes you to the Google search results page.

- **Tab Button** - Because you are limited in space, you don't actually see all your tabs like you would on a normal browser; instead you get a button that tells you how many tabs are open. If you tap it, you can either toggle between the tabs, or swipe over one of the pages to close the tab.

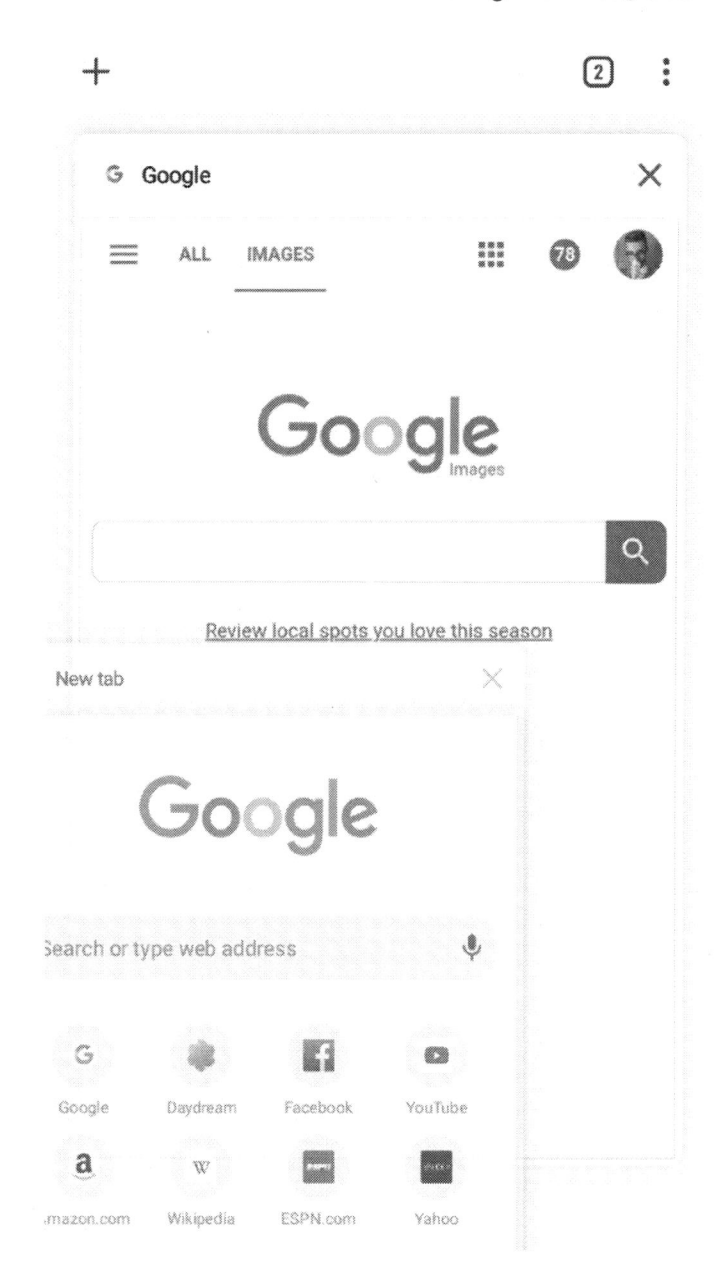

- **Menu Button** - The last button brings up a menu with a series of other options that I'll talk about next.

Scott La Counte

→ ☆ ⬇ ⓘ ↻

New tab

New incognito tab

Bookmarks

Recent tabs

History

Downloads

Share…

Find in page

Add to Home screen

Desktop site ☐

Settings

Help & feedback

The menu is pretty straightforward, but there are a few things worth noting.

"New incognito tab" opens your phone into private browsing; that doesn't mean your IP isn't tracked. It means your history isn't record; it also means passwords and cookies aren't stored.

A little bit further down is "History"; if you want your history erased so there's no record on your phone of where you went, then go here, and clear your browsing history.

History

Your Google Account may have other forms of browsing history at myactivity.google.com.

CLEAR BROWSING DATA...

If you want to erase more than just websites (passwords, for example) then go to "Settings" at the very bottom of the menu. This opens up more advance settings.

Scott La Counte

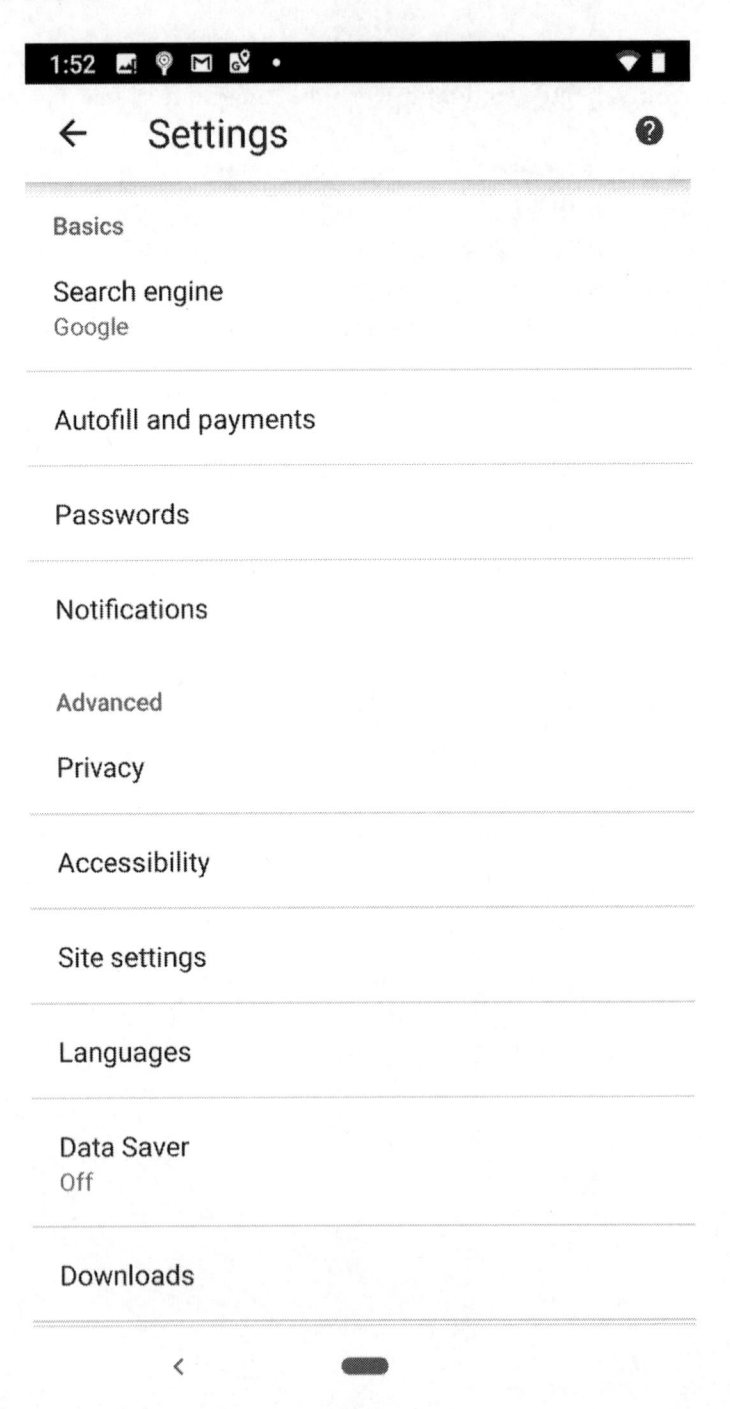

← Settings

Basics

Search engine
Google

Autofill and payments

Passwords

Notifications

Advanced

Privacy

Accessibility

Site settings

Languages

Data Saver
Off

Downloads

6 /
snap it!

THE CAMERA IS the bread and butter of the Pixel phone. Many people consider the Pixel to be the greatest camera ever on a phone. I'll leave that for you to decide.

One of the nice things about photos on the Pixel is it stores them online automatically, so you don't have to worry about losing them. You can see them by logging into the Google account associated with your Pixel and going here:

https://photos.google.com

Best of all: this is all free! You don't have to pay extra for more storage and it doesn't go against other things in your Google Drive.

To make sure you have this feature on, go to "Settings" and "Backup" and "sync"; make sure you toggle it on.

There are some caveats (such as the photos may be compressed), so read the terms.

the basics

Are you ready to get your Ansel Adams on? Let's get started by opening the Camera app. You can do this several ways:

- The most obvious is to tap the Camera on your favorite bar or by swiping up and opening it from all apps. It looks like a camera—go figure!

- Double press the power button.

Once you are in the app, don't forget, you can twist the phone to toggle between selfie mode.

When you open the app, it starts in the basic camera mode. The UI can look pretty simple, but don't be fooled. There are a lot of controls.

The first is at the top. Tap the down arrow at the top of the screen.

The options are pretty straightforward, but "Top Shot" (which used to be called Motion) might be new to you. This is basically like a very short video of your photo. You can turn it on for all photos, auto so it turns on when motion is detected, or turn it off. Top Shot is larger, so storing it in this mode will take a little more space. Night Sight is ideal for when you in low light. The screen below is the basic camera settings, but this menu can differ slightly depending on what camera mode you are in.

Mastering the Pixel 9 and Pixel 9 Pro

| More light | | | |
| Night Sight | 🚫 | 🌙ᴬ | ⚡ |

| Top Shot | | | |
| Disabled ⓘ | 🚫 | Ⓐ | ⬤ |

| Timer | | | |
| Off | 🚫 | ③ | ⑩ |

| Ratio | | | |
| Full image (4:3) | | ▢ | ▢ |

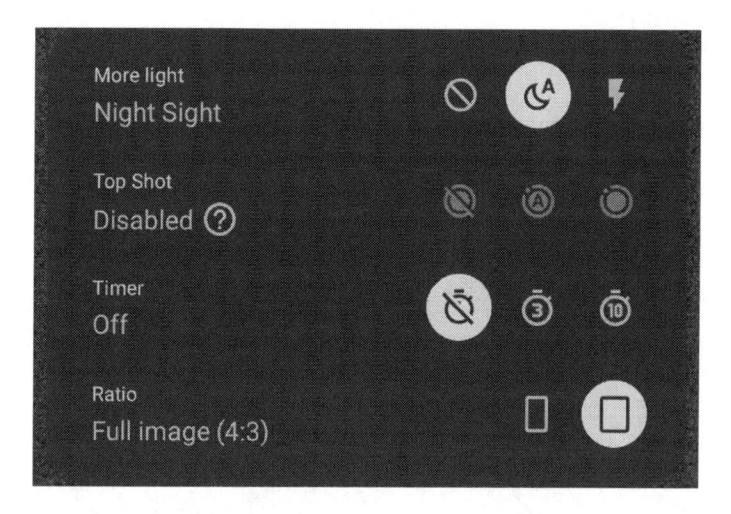

Over on the upper right side is the folder icon; that lets you pick where you will save the photo you are currently shooting.

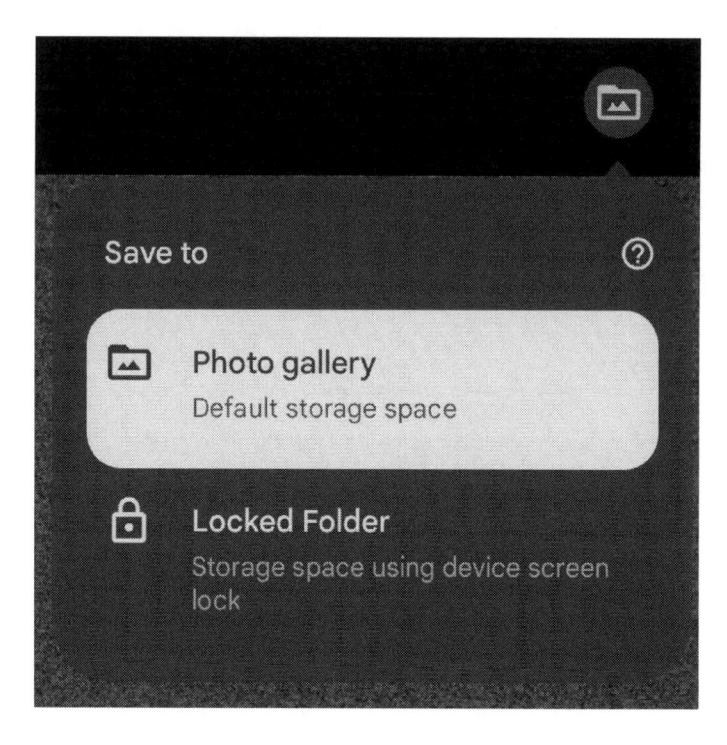

Save to

📷 **Photo gallery**
Default storage space

🔒 **Locked Folder**
Storage space using device screen lock

On the bottom of the screen are all the modes and the shutter. Starting

159

Scott La Counte

with the top row from the left you have the selfie button, the shutter, and the last photo preview (tapping that will show all of your photos that you have taken starting with the most recent). On the bottom, you have the camera modes, which I'll cover in more detail later in this chapter.

When you point your camera at a product and tap and hold over that product, this will activate Google Lens, which will try to detect what you are pointing at and give you more information about it. It's not always 100% accurate (for example, I pointed it at the Pixel 5 case and it showed me info for the Pixel 3), but it's still a nice feature.

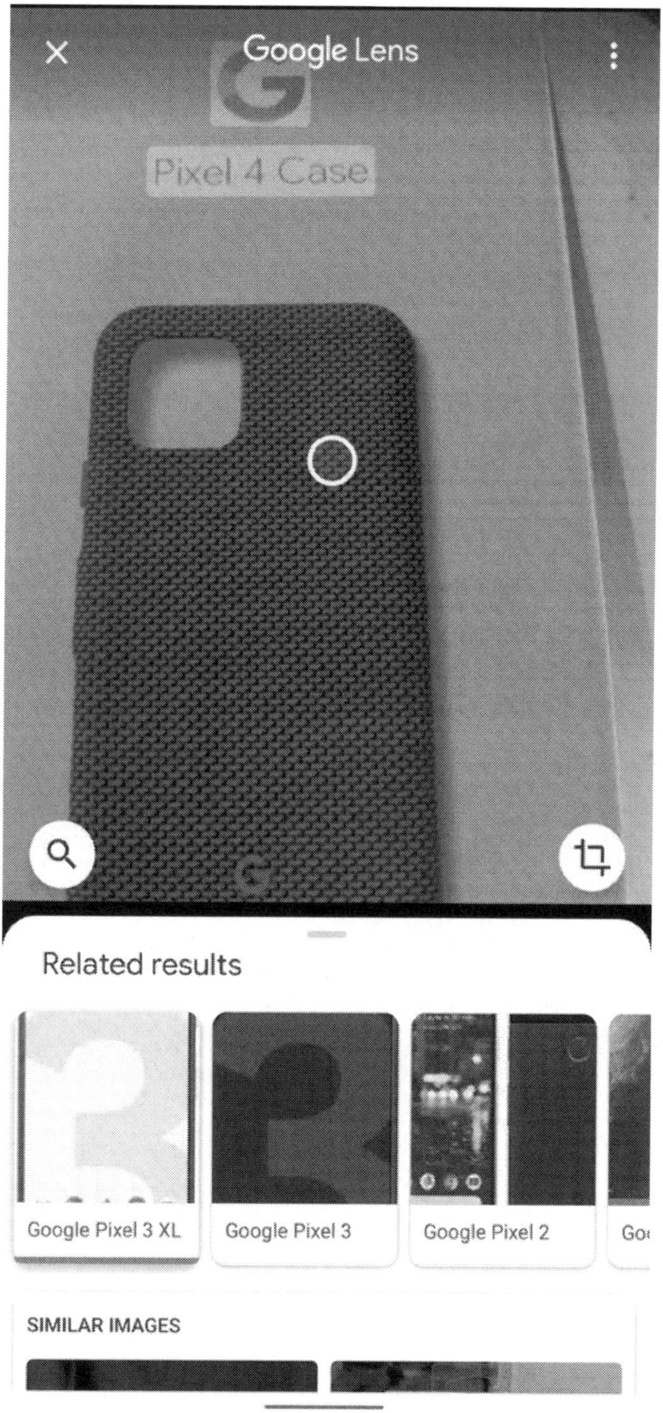
Google Lens
Pixel 4 Case
Related results
Google Pixel 3 XL
Google Pixel 3
Google Pixel 2
SIMILAR IMAGES

If you tap once, but don't hold, this will bring up exposure and zoom options (you can also pinch in and out to zoom). Tapping on the area of the screen that you want to focus on will also focus on that area; for example, if you point it at a group of people in front of a crowd of people, you can tap the group to tell the camera that's the focus of the show.

When you tap in the middle of the screen as you prepare to take a shot, you can use the sliders to control the amount of brightness, contrast or warmth the photo has.

One final thing I will point out about taking pictures. Remember up in the top bar (when you swipe down), there's an option to disable the camera or mic? Well you sort of need those things to take photos and videos, right? If you try and do it when they're on, you'll get the message below. Tap the unlock button to enable the features.

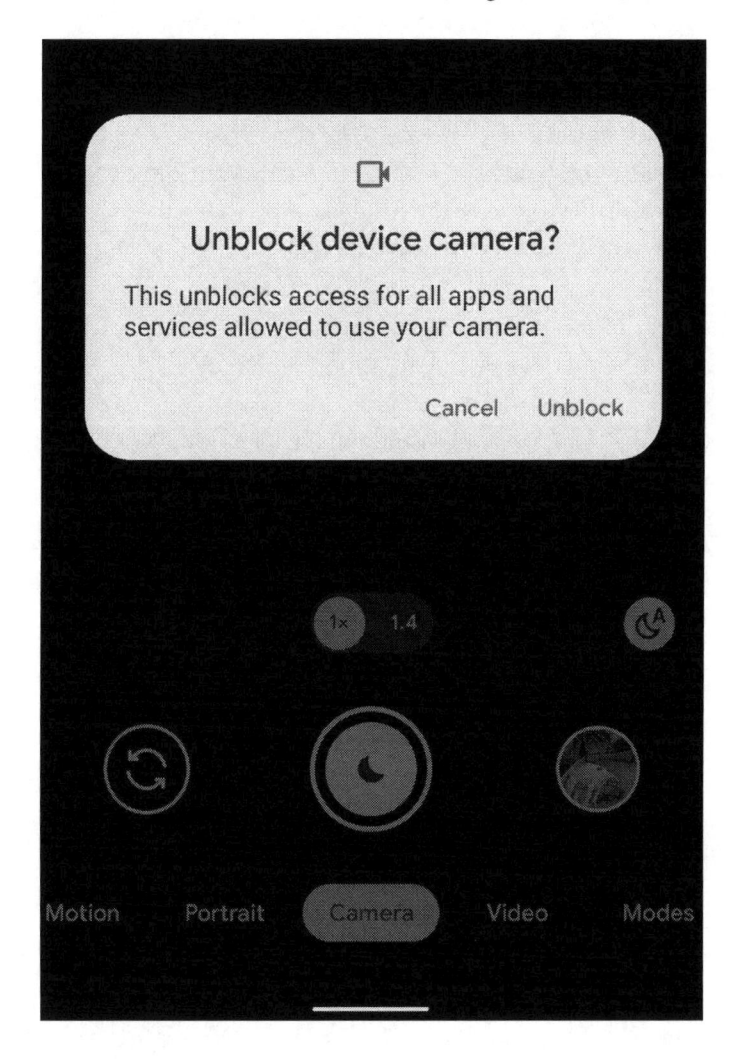

hello (photo) friend

Do you have people you take photos of more than others? A kid? A partner? A friend? A pet? Google's AI can prioritize people you photograph most. To turn it on go to the Camera app, open the settings and enable Frequent Faces.

camera modes

Let's look at each of the modes next.

Think of modes like different lenses. You have your basic camera lens, but then you can also have a lens for fisheye, and close up. If you look at the bottom of your camera app, you can slide left and right to get to the different modes. In 2019, Google added Night Sight mode, which helps you capture better photos at night. It works like the basic Camera mode. It also turns on automatically when it detects you are shooting in night.

Next to Night Sight is Portrait mode. Portrait mode gives your photos a sharp professional look to them. It blurs the background to really make your photos pop. I'll show an example with a photo of myself—apologies in advance for my looks!

Here I am with zero blur:

And here I am with maximum blur:

So how do you do that? First, slide to the Portrait mode. The phone will try to figure out where the focal point will be, but you'll get the best effect if you tap on the screen where the focus will be. If you tap on the face, for example, it will tell the phone you want to blur everything else. The change won't be noticeable—you can edit it after.

I'll show you how to edit that blur a little later in this section.

Video mode takes, you guessed it, videos! Once you tap record, there are not as many settings as the camera. To the left, there's a pause button, the middle is the stop button, and the far right is the camera shutter—that means as you are recording you can still take photos.

When you tap to focus on a subject, you'll notice that there's only a slider for zoom (bottom), and brightness (right side); there's also a lock to lock in on your focus.

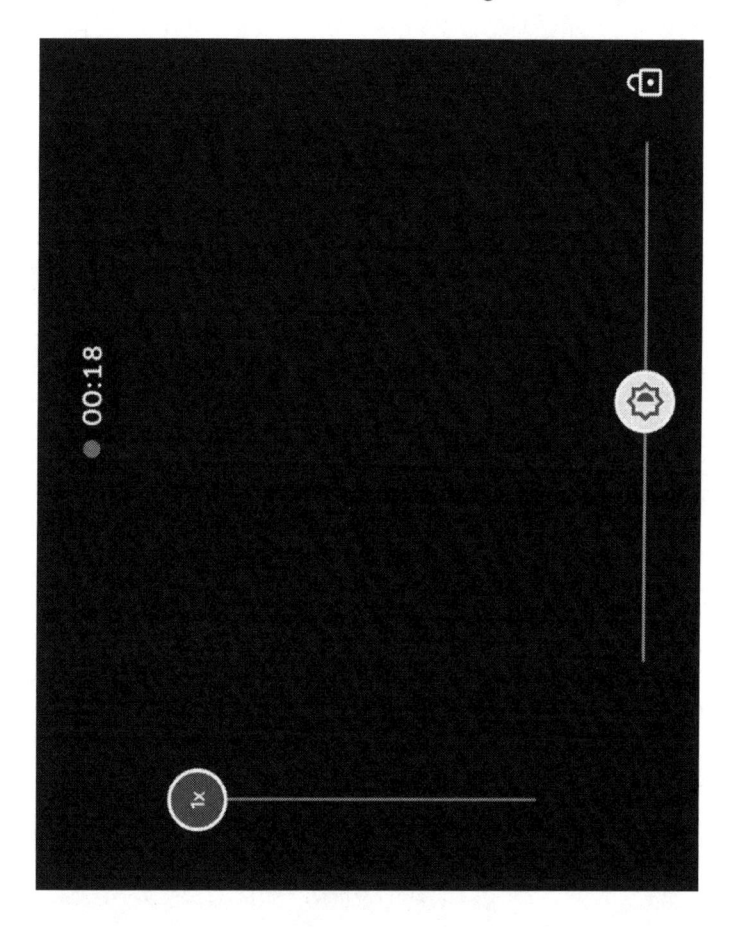

There's also a Cinematic video mode that takes videos with the blurred effected—only the main person in the scene is in focus.

Before you shoot a video, there's also an option to toggle between Slow Motion, Normal, and Time Lapse; if you are coming to the Pixel 5 from an earlier model, you'll probably be used to using these modes in another place; they used to be located under "More." Google decided to eliminate that extra step and put all the video modes in one place.

Scott La Counte

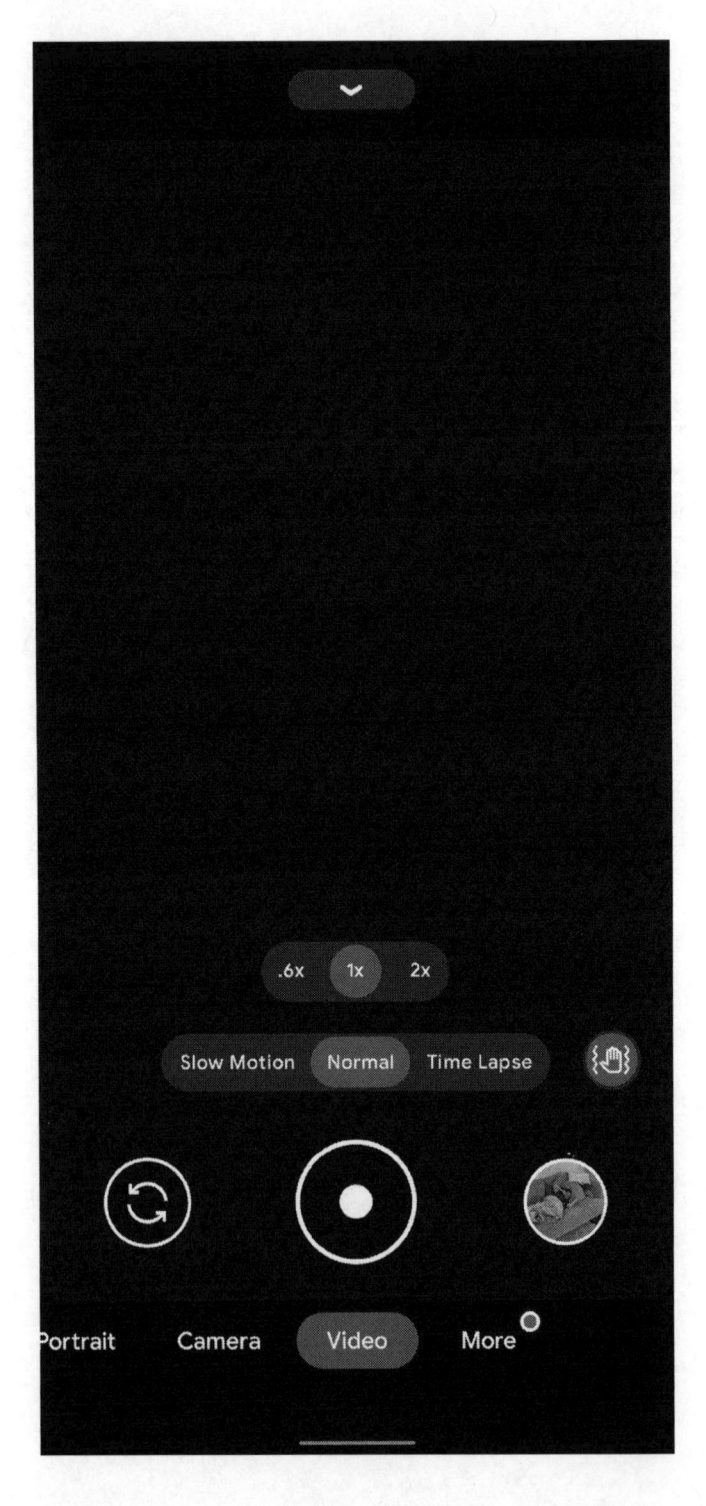

So speaking of this "More" area, let's tap on that next and see the other modes available. There's three more: Panorama, Photo Sphere, and Lens. The modes can take good photos, but they are more fun modes.

Panorama is great for landscape photos. The below photo is an example (note: this was not shot on the Pixel):

The way it works on the Pixel, is you take one photo, and then you move a little to the right and take another, and so on and so forth; then all of those photos are stitched together to make one giant photo. Just hit the arrow button for each photo and the blue button to finish (or X button to cancel).

Photo Sphere is sort of like a panorama photo; it's several photos stitched together. But where a panorama is straight, Photo Sphere is 360 degrees; it's fun for your phone or sharing online (like Facebook). To use it, tap the shutter when in Photo Sphere mode, then move your camera up and down, and left and right.

Mastering the Pixel 9 and Pixel 9 Pro

Before you take the photo, you can also tap the down arrow at the top of the screen and change the shape.

When you view the photo, you can either use your finger to move the direction of it, or you can tap the VR mode in the lower right corner and use VR headsets.

Mastering the Pixel 9 and Pixel 9 Pro

The last mode is Lens. I already mentioned how you can activate it in the regular camera mode, but there are more features in the native Lens mode.

You can do automatic, but there are modes within this mode to translate, scan a doc, look for consumer products, or identify food. By default, it's on the automatic mode (the middle one), but tapping on the other icons will switch the mode and give you more accurate results.

Most modes have unique settings. Translate, for example, lets you auto-detect the language you are scanning, or change it to something different.

173

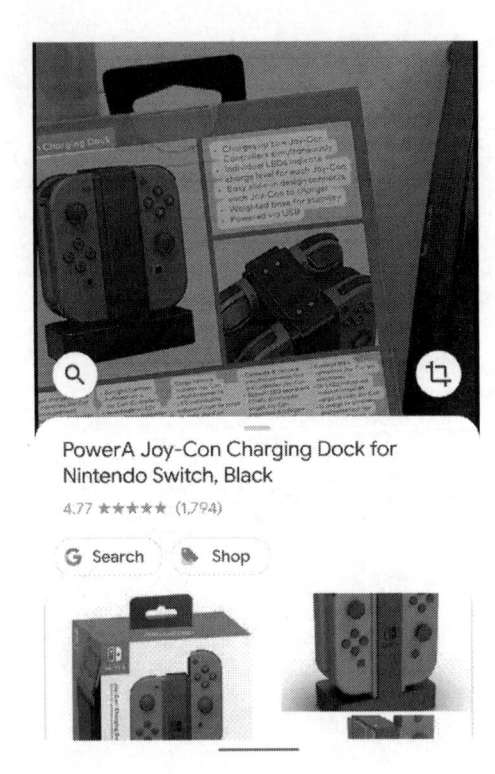

Depending on what you scan, it will give you information about the product, and you can click for more information.

Mastering the Pixel 9 and Pixel 9 Pro

editing photo

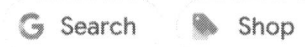

Editing photos is one of the many places that Good really shines. This is where AI really takes over—you can remove people from photos, move them to different places, change their expressions, and even change a bright sunny day into something dreary.

You can access editing by opening the photo you want to make edits to.

This is done by either opening it from the camera app by clicking on the photo preview (next to the shutter);

Or by opening the Photo app.

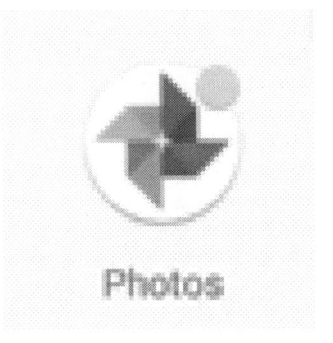

When you open a photo, the first thing you'll want to do is tap the Edit button.

The top row is your menu options. Below the options, you'll see all the menus. The first thing that comes up is always Suggestions; this is always dynamic. It changes based on how the AI thinks it can make the photo better. Sometimes it's spot on. Sometimes…not so much.

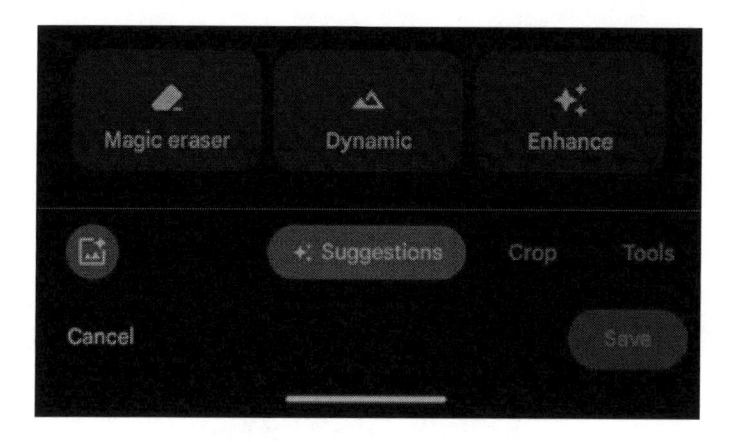

Magic Editor

One of the big features of Pixel is the Magic Editor. This uses AI to let you make huge tweaks to a photo—for example, you can move someone standing on a beach but not by the water, to the waters edge.

It's AI and sometimes works better than others. You'll probably notice in some photos edges and other markings that make it clear that the photo is not 100% real. It really depends on the photo.

You also might not see the option right away; if you have a brand new phone, make sure you do all the updates—both phone updates and app updates.

So let's try it out. To get started tap the Magic Edit button in the lower left side of the screen.

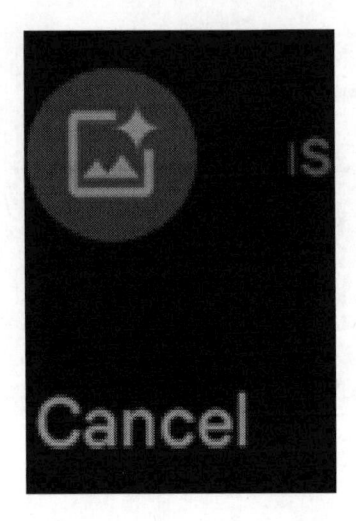

It will take a few seconds to load, so be patient. For this example, I'm going to take an old wedding photo—yes, you can make edits to older photo (in the example below, the photo is 15 years old); I'm going to move myself from the left side of the bench to the right side.

Mastering the Pixel 9 and Pixel 9 Pro

The first thing I'll do is circle what I want to move—it doesn't have to be precise.

After a few seconds, you'll see a white shadow around what Google thinks you want to move.

You can now drag the portion of the image wherever you want it to go.

Mastering the Pixel 9 and Pixel 9 Pro

As you drag it, you can also pinch outward to make the image bigger or smaller.

When you are satisfied with where the image is going to be placed, let go and tap the checkmark in the lower right corner. The image will start regenerating. It will take a few seconds.

181

When it's done, it will have several photos to toggle through, and you can pick the best one. You can see in the image below that it's not perfect; in my example, a shadow has been left where I was previously seated. If you aren't happy, try again—circling something else—or try another photo.

Sky Tool

Another feature promoted is the ability to change the sky in a photo. It's not quite night and day, but it still is pretty cool.

If you go to Tools on a photo with a background that's outdoor, you should see the Sky option. Tap that. In my example, I'm going to change a very bright sky to something more dreary.

It's not a drastic change, but you can see how it does look more overcast now.

The tools menu also gives you the option to apply a blur effect to a photo. So I can put the focus on me and not that structure in the background.

And, I'll point out again, this is an older photo—it was taken over ten years ago on an iPhone. I say that to make it clear that you can use whatever photo—shot from whatever device—that you want.

Magic Eraser

Tools also has one of the newest and most exciting features: Magic Erase. Want to erase the photobomber from the image? Done! That old high school sweetheart who broke your heart? Gone!

Before talking more about this magic eraser tool, let me briefly mention that if you are editing a portrait photo, you'll see even more options (see image below).

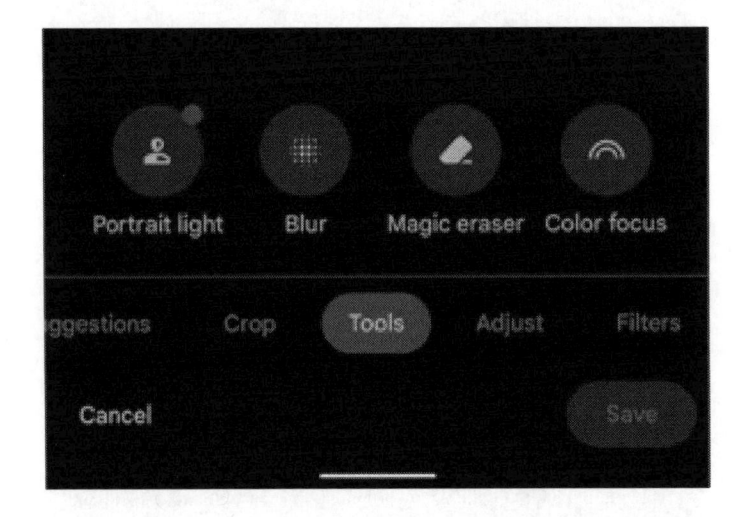

This is where you can change the focus of the image (so you can blur something else), adjust the lighting, or reduce the amount of blur.

But back to that core feature: magic erase. How does it work? Let's take a look. The image below is great, isn't it?! But I don't like that statue on the left.

Mastering the Pixel 9 and Pixel 9 Pro

To remove her, I go into Edit > Tools, select Magic eraser.

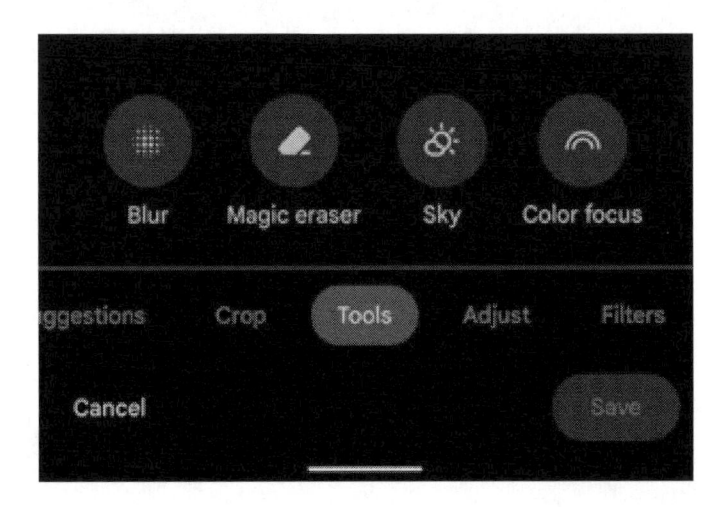

From here, I just rub my finger on the area that I want to erase.

When I'm done, I lift my finger. Poof. She's all gone!

Mastering the Pixel 9 and Pixel 9 Pro

Scott La Counte

Pretty cool, right? Make sure and tap Done and save it.

If by chance you don't see this feature, then you probably need to update your phone. Also, remember, this feature is currently only available on the Pixel.

Other Adjustments

Next to Tools is the Adjust button. This is where you can manually adjust things like brightness. Suggestions will also do this, but it will do it automatically.

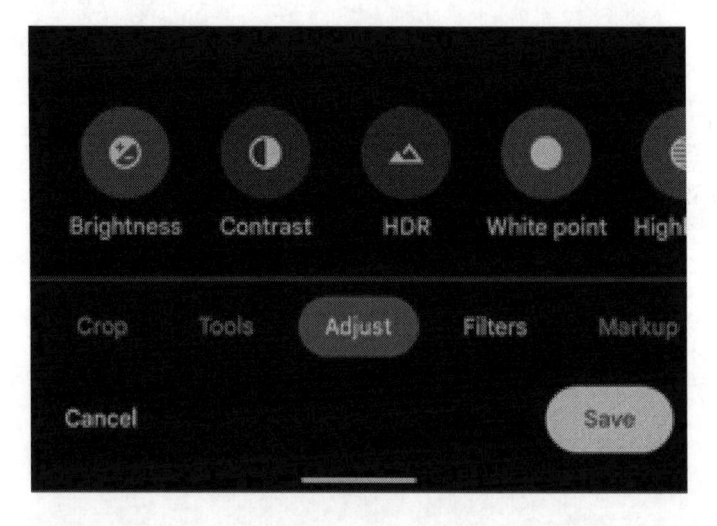

Clicking on any of the settings will bring up a new slighter; move it left or right to adjust the intensity.

Mastering the Pixel 9 and Pixel 9 Pro

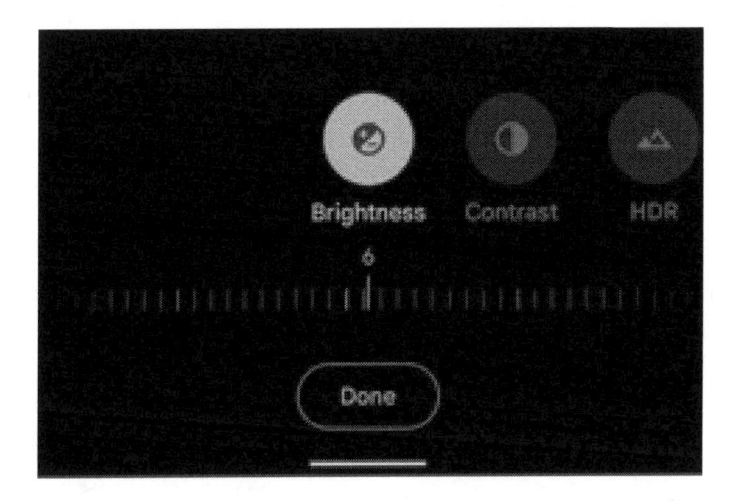

Filters is the next setting, and it will automatically apply a filter over the photo. So if you want it to have a Vivid look—i.e. one that's full of bright colors, then tap the Vivid filter.

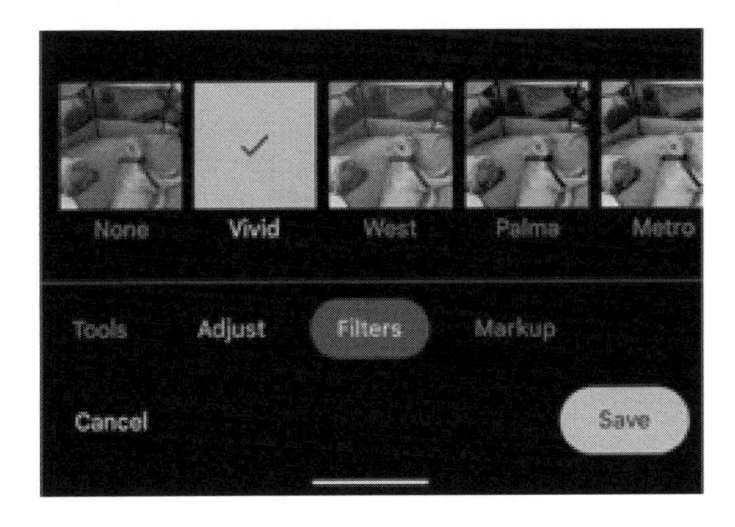

The last setting is Markup. This setting is used to write text or highlight things in the photo. For example, if you want to circle something in the photo that you are trying to point out to someone.

191

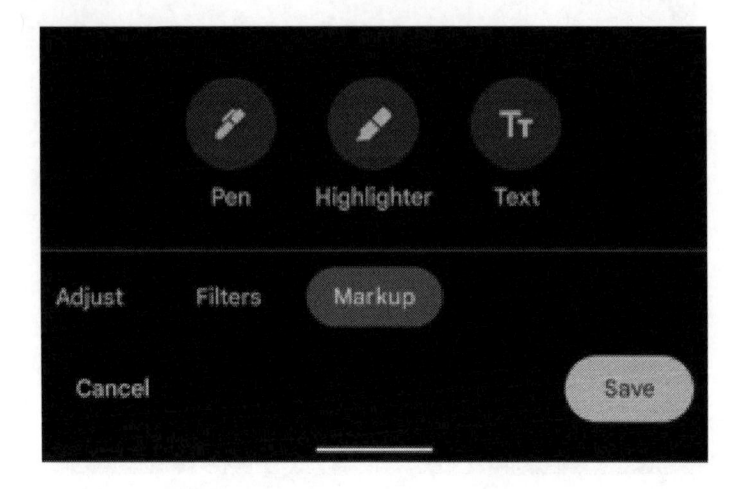

Blurred Photos

Google's AI really helps photos shine. The unblur feature shows you the full potential of this AI engine; it can take previously blurry photos and sharpen them.

It's under Tools and says Unblur. Tap that once, and it will automatically make the adjustment that it thinks is appropriate for the photo.

Mastering the Pixel 9 and Pixel 9 Pro

Once the adjustment is made, you'll see a slider that lets you make more adjustments—100 is the max you can go; going down would in values would make the photo more blurry.

Mastering the Pixel 9 and Pixel 9 Pro

organizing your photos

The great thing about mobile photos is you always have a camera ready to capture memorable events; the bad thing about mobile photos is you always have a camera ready to capture events, and you'll find you have hundreds and hundreds of photos very quickly.

Fortunately, Google makes it very simple to organize your photos so you can find what you are looking for.

Let's open up the Photos app and see how to get things organized.

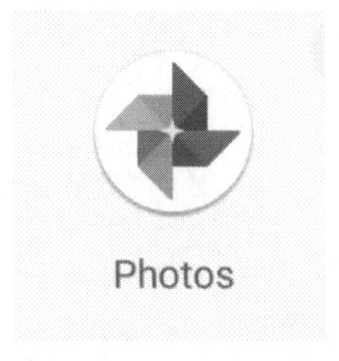

Pixel keeps things pretty simple by having only four options on the bottom of your screen.

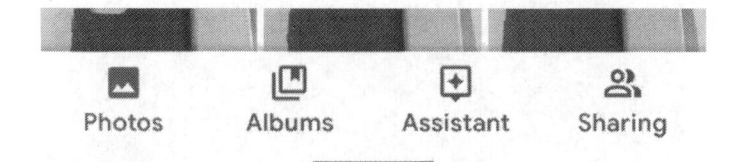

In the upper right corner, there's three dots, which is the photo option menu; that menu is there no matter where you are in the Photo app.

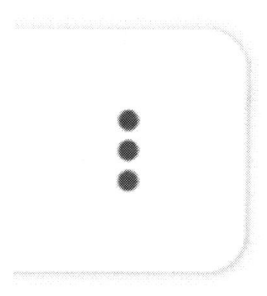

When you tap that menu, you'll get several more options.

- Select
- Layout

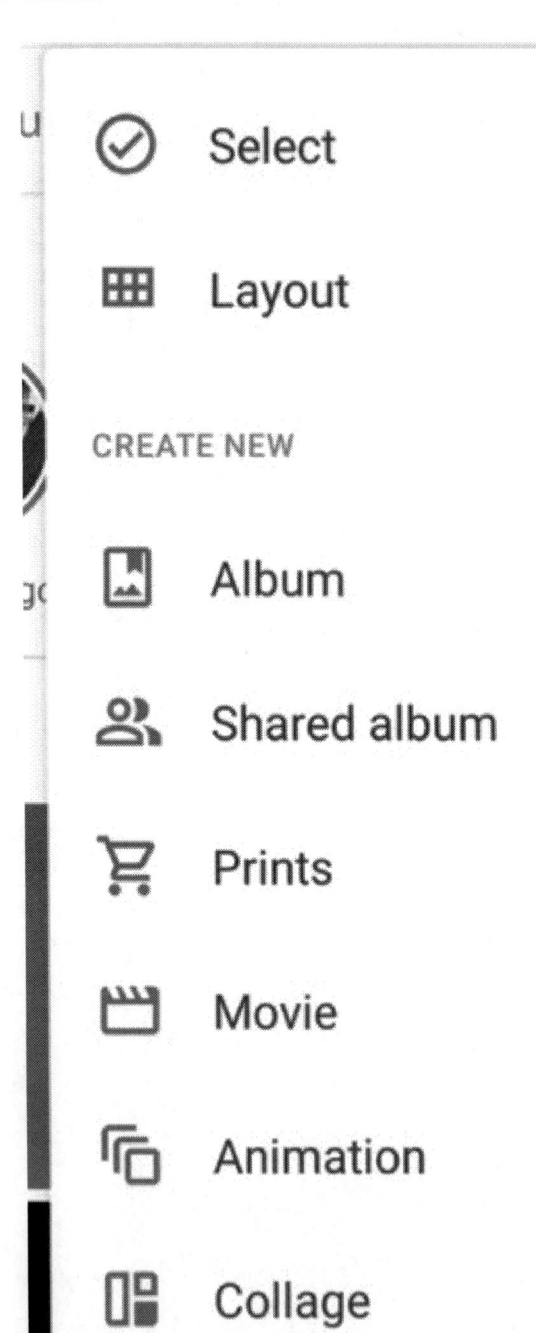

CREATE NEW

- Album
- Shared album
- Prints
- Movie
- Animation
- Collage

The options are as follows:

- Select – This lets you select photos on your screen so you can share, email, print, and more.
- Layout – There are two Layout modes: Comfortable view (this view creates a grid with small and large photo thumbnails) and Month view (all thumbnails are the same size).

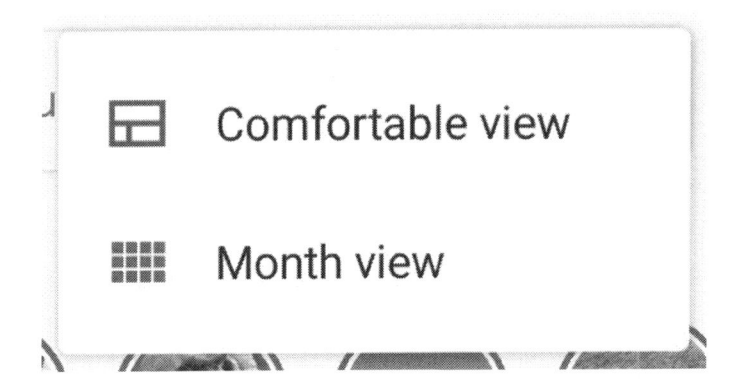

- Album – Let's you create an album by selecting photos or faces.

- Shared album – Lets you share albums.
- Prints – Quickly create photo albums that you can print and have sent to your house.

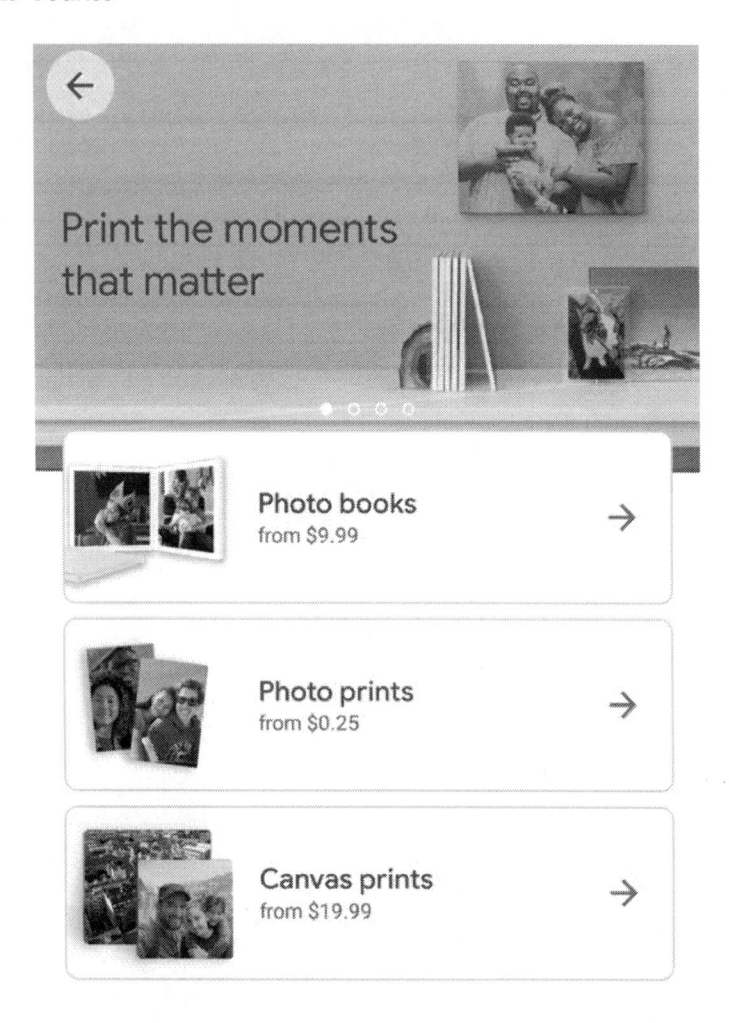

- Movie – Movies lets you create video memories of your photos. You can either select "New movie" and create one based on selected photos or pick from one of the many templates. It can take several minutes for movies to generate when you pick this option.

✕ Create movie

New movie
Select photos & videos

They Grow Up So Fast
Watch a child grow up right before your eyes

Meow Movie
The internet needs more cat videos

Doggie Movie
A movie that celebrates man's best friend

In Loving Memory
Celebrate the life of someone who has passed away

Selfie Movie
Finally, something to do with all those selfies!

- Animation – Animation is kind of like a .gif; whereas movies could run for several minutes, animations are only a few seconds.
- Collage – Collage lets you pick up to nine photos to combine into one collage. If you pick less, Google will automatically arrange it for you. The below is an example of three photos in a collage. There isn't a lot of customization here, so if you want a collage, you might want to download a free collage app that has a few more tools in it.

In the upper left corner is three lines; this opens your second menu option screen.

Some of the options (such as buy prints) are the same ones you've already seen in the other menu.

	Print store	
🛒	Photo books, prints, and canvas	
🖼	Photo frames	NEW
📁	Device folders	
⤓	Archive	
🗑	Trash	
📱	Free up space	
⚙	Settings	

GOOGLE APPS

	PhotoScan	↗

	Help & feedback	

Photo frames is an option available if you have a Google Nest Hub (or Google Hub). This lets you pick the photos that display on your Hub.

← **Photo frames**

Get started with your first photo frame. Once set up, you can manage the albums it displays here.

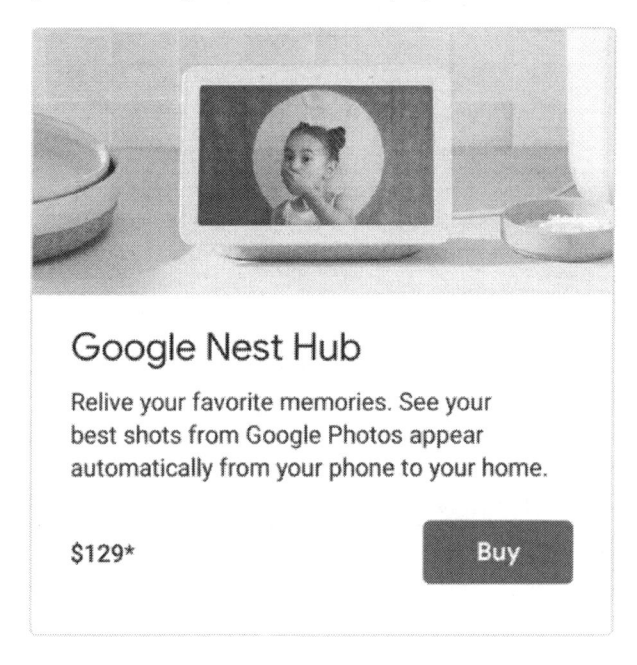

Google Nest Hub

Relive your favorite memories. See your best shots from Google Photos appear automatically from your phone to your home.

$129*   Buy

*Terms apply.

Device folders is where you can find screenshots if you've taken any. You can take a screenshot by pressing the orange button and the down volume button at the same time.

Archive is to help you declutter your phone. You can archive photos so your main photo area has less photos; archiving them puts them here, but they will still be searchable.

Clear the clutter

Archived items will be kept here. They'll still show in albums & search results.

Learn More

If you delete a photo, it is actually not permanently deleted from your device...yet. It is moved here. This is helpful if you have a kid who likes to delete things! If you tap any of the photos, you can restore it or delete it—deleting it means it's gone for good.

"Free up space" removes photos from your device and backs them up to your Google account. You can still view them whenever you want.

Settings will be covered in the next sections.

Finally, PhotoScan is a free app that you have to download to use; the app lets you use your Pixel camera to scan old print photos. It works surprisingly well and is recommended if you have lots of photos that you want saved.

PhotoScan by Google Photos
Google LLC

4.3 ★
89K reviews

10M+
Downloads

E
Everyone

Install

The next tab on the bottom of the Photos app (Albums) is where you can go to start grouping your photos together. There are already things like Places and Things that have albums; if you have starred anything, you'll also see one for Favorites.

What you might not know is Google is quietly working in the background to figure out who is in photos. Once you take several photos, you'll see one called People & Pets.

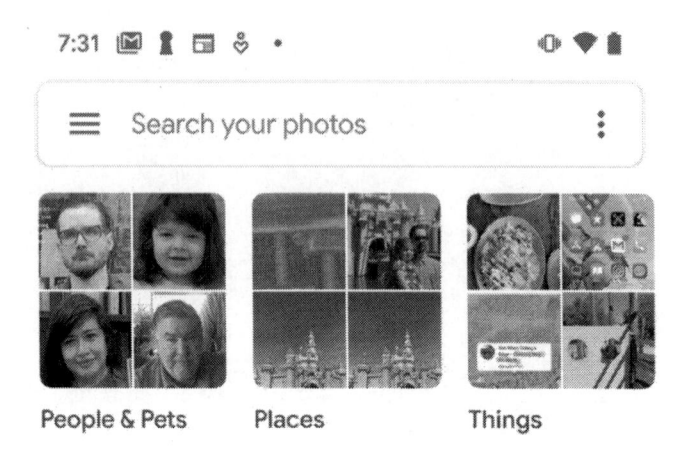

When you open it, you'll see people you probably recognize, and when you click on it, it will show you other photos that they are in. Pretty cool, right? What's cooler is you can name those people, so you can search more easily for them. Just click their face, then tap "Add a name." In the example below, Google has found my dog's face.

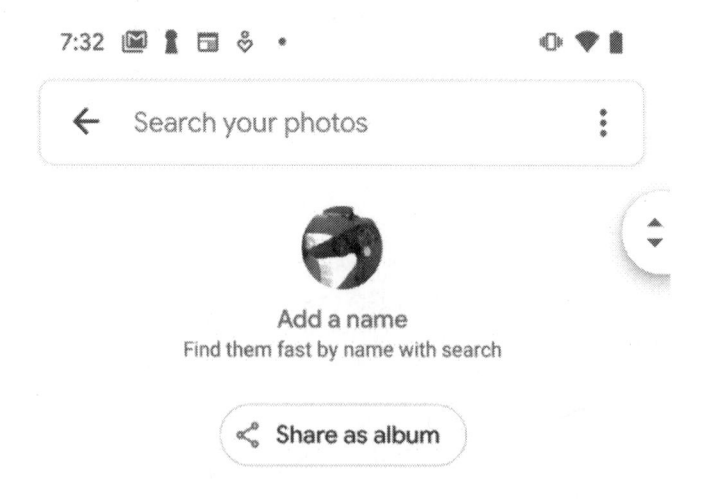

I added her name, so when I go back, I now see her photo with her name. I can now search for photos using her name. You can also search for photos using names of places or even foods or things. The photo search is pretty smart, and it gets even smarter as you take more photos.

When you want to create a new album, just click the three dots in the upper right corner.

It will ask you to name it; you can pick whatever you want. From here, you can either auto select things based on people and pets, or you can select your own photos.

Scott La Counte

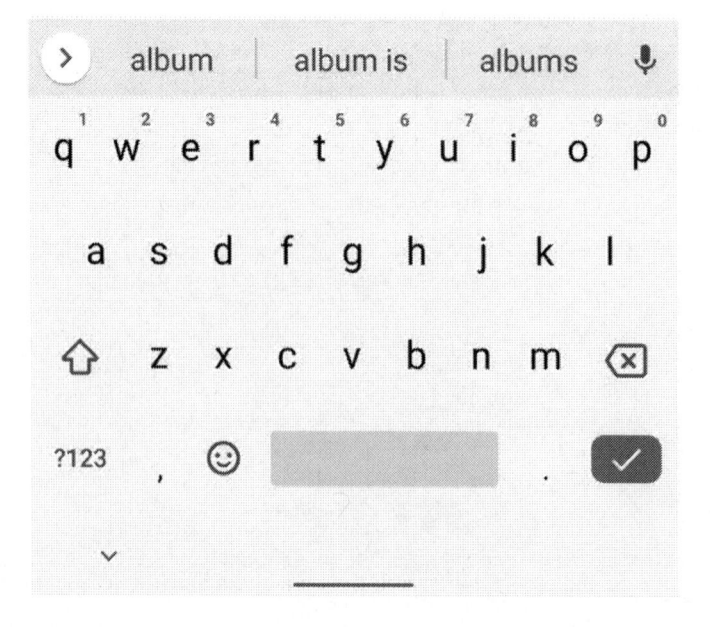

If you select photos on your own, you'll just have to manually tap each one that you want in the album.

If you select to have it auto create, you'll just have to pick what you want to use (a person's name, for example).

Once the album is created, you can tap the three dots in the upper right corner to add more photos, order photos, delete the album, or share.

Select

Edit album

Options

Order photos

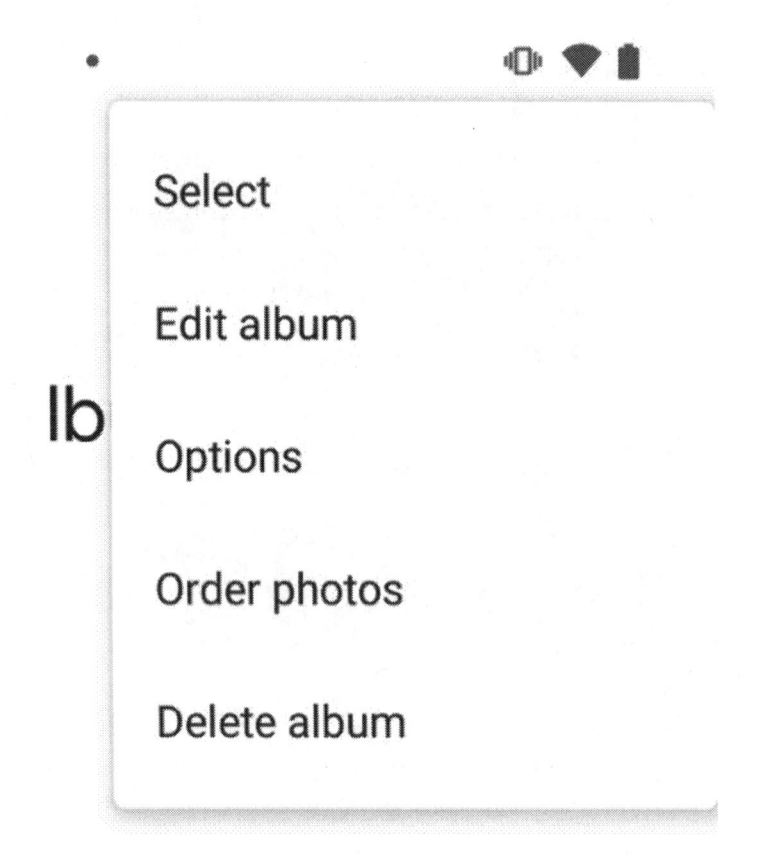

Delete album

You can also click the Share button on the album (or on any photo), which brings up the Sharing menu. You can share with a link, via email, Bluetooth, text message, and more.

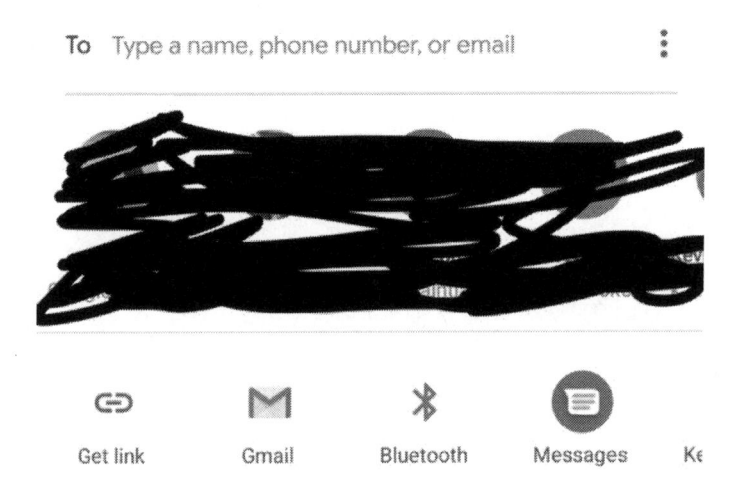

The Assistant option is recommendations from Google's AI bot; it collects memories based on places you've been and groups together what it considers the best shots.

The last option on the bottom menu is Sharing. Sharing lets you select other people who can see your photos. You can, for example, share all photos of a certain person with that person, and you can set it to share new photos of that person whenever you take them.

To get started, just tap the "Add partner account."

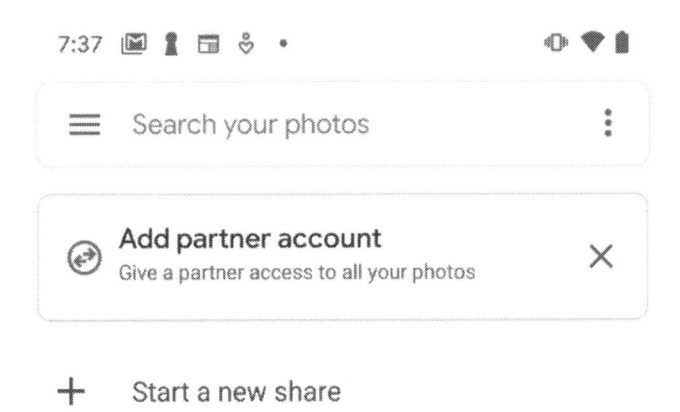

Next you'll see a screen telling you what sharing is. Tap the blue "Get Started" option.

7:37

Share your library

1. Select your partner
2. Choose what you want to share

Get Started

Learn more

From here you'll search for the person's name or email; Google might also have a few suggested contacts for you, and you can just tap their name.

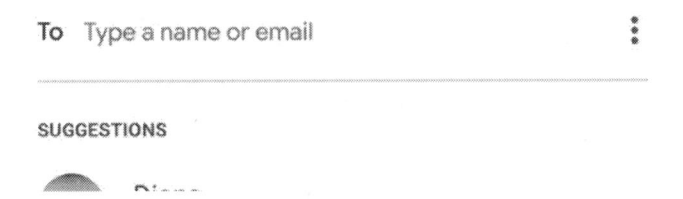

Once you pick the person, it will ask you what you want to share. You can share every single photo now, and in the future, or you can pick certain people or days.

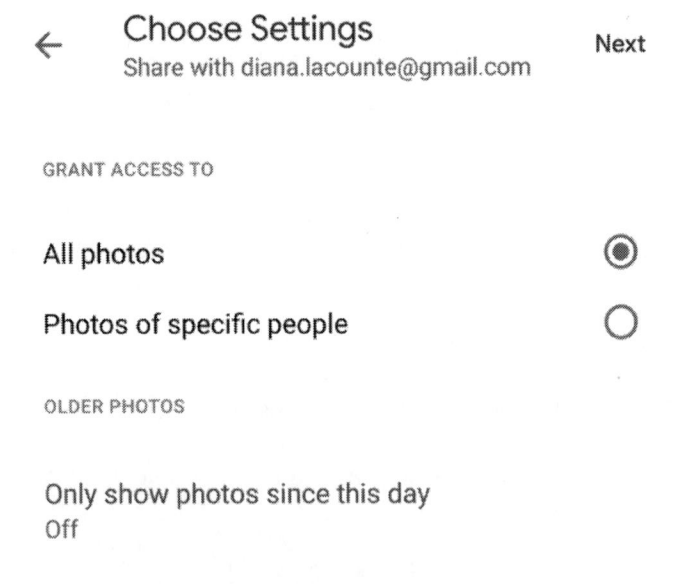

It will confirm what you are sharing before it shares; once you tap "Send invitation," it will email an invite to that person and they have to accept it before they actually see the photos.

✓ All of your photos

✓ Including older photos

New photos will be shared automatically. Learn more

Send invitation

settings

You probably won't spend a lot of time in Photo settings, but they're still good to know for those occasions when you do want to make changes.

You can access your settings by opening the Photo app, tapping on the three lines in the upper left corner, then tapping on Settings.

Free up device storage
Remove original photos & videos from your device that are already backed up

Notifications
Manage preferences for notifications

Group similar faces
Manage preferences for face grouping

Assistant cards
Choose the types of cards to show

Memories
Manage what you see in your memories

SHARING

Shared libraries
diana.lacounte@gmail.com

Remove video from motion photos
Share only the still photos when sharing by link & in albums

Remove geo location
From photos & videos that you share by link, but not by other means

There are three areas of the settings: Main, Sharing, and Google apps.

Main settings

- Back up & sync – Lets you pick how photos are backed up (what email account they are linked to, the resolution of the photos, when to back them up, where to back them up, and more).
- Free up device storage – Removes photos from your device and stores them in your account so you have more room for additional photos.
- Notifications – Lets you pick the kinds of pop up notifications you'll receive regarding photos (suggested sharing, printing promotions, photo book drafts, suggested photo books).
- Group similar faces – Turn on and off face grouping; if you don't want a robot scanning your photos to figure out the person that's in the shot, you can disable it here.
- Assistant cards – Picks the cards that show up in the Assistant menu of the Photos app (Creations, Rediscover this day, Recent highlights, Suggested Rotations, Suggested Archive).
- Memories – Memories are usually fun; seeing Google show you a photo of your kid as a baby can put a smile on your face as you start your day. But sometimes memories can suck—you go through a messy divorce or a loved one dies, and Google is there to remind you of their face. You can take those people out of your memories here. It doesn't delete them from your account; you just won't see them show up in your feed.

Sharing Settings

- Shared libraries – Lets you see who can view your photos.
- Remove video from motion photos – Motion photos are nice—they're also big. If you prefer to just show the photo and not the video clip that goes with it, you can turn it off here.
- Remove geo location – Your photos have geo tags on them (unless you turn them off); that means when you share a photo, it might have things like your home address. If you don't want people to see that, then you can disable geo location with the people you are sharing it with.

Google apps

- Google Location settings – Lets you pick what apps can see your photos.
- Google Lens – Not a setting as much as instructions about how to use the app.

7 /
going beyond

IF YOU WANT to take total control of your Pixel, then you need to know where the system settings are and what can and can't be changed there.

First the easy part: the system settings are located with the rest of your apps. Swipe up, and scroll down to "Settings."

There's a lot of settings here. Below are the available ones:

- Network & Internet

- Connected devices
- Apps
- Notification
- Battery
- Storage
- Sound & Vibration
- Display
- Wallpaper & Style
- Accessibility
- Privacy
- Location
- Safety & emergency
- Security
- Passwords & Accounts
- Digital Wellbeing & parental control
- Google
- System
- About phone
- Tips & support

I'll cover what each setting does in this chapter.

network & internet

This setting, like most settings, does exactly what it sounds like: connects to the Internet. If you need to connect to a new wireless connection (or disconnect from one) you can do it here. Tapping on the current wireless lets you see other networks, and the toggle lets you switch it on and off.

4:04

Network & internet

Internet
Proverbs_17:22

Calls & SMS
No SIM

SIMs
Add a network

Airplane mode

Hotspot & tethering
Off

Data Saver
Off

VPN
None

Private DNS
Automatic

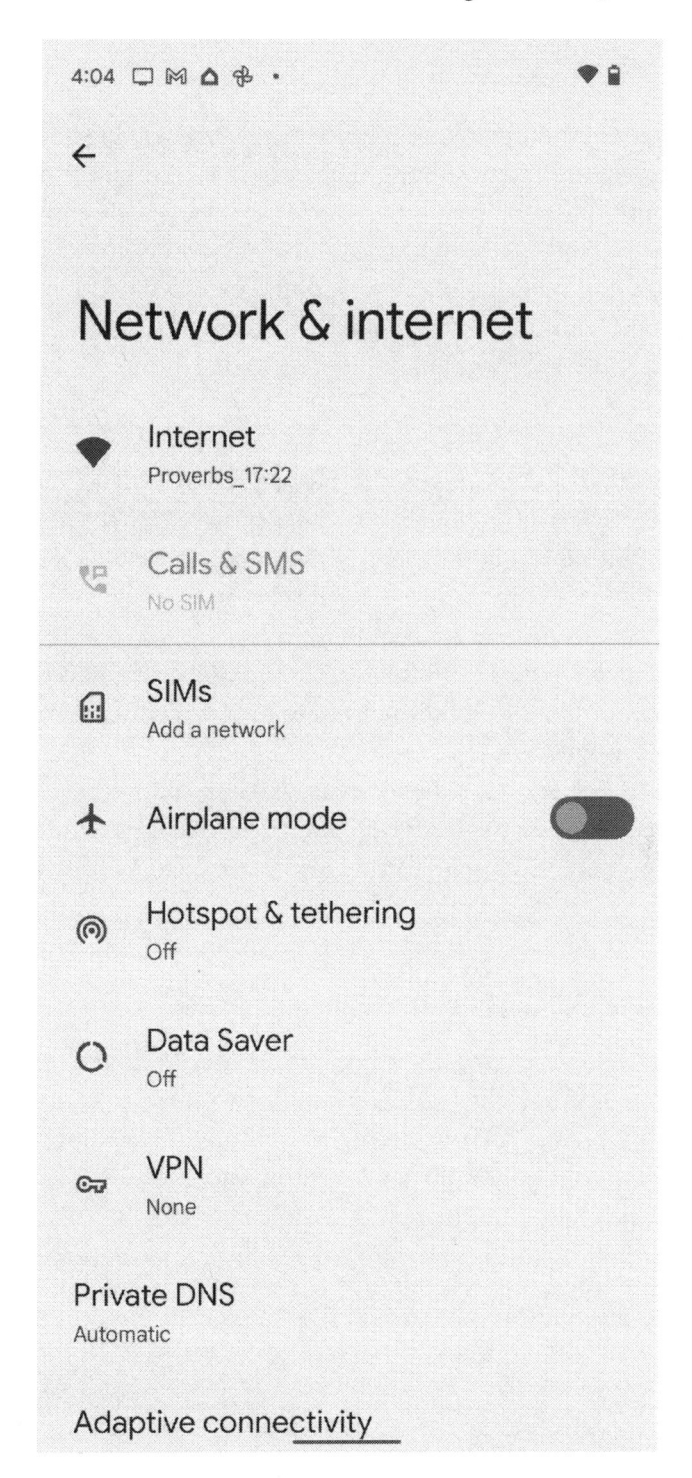

Adaptive connectivity

Mobile network is for your carrier (Verizon, AT&T, Sprint, etc.).

Data usage tells you how much data you've used; tapping on it gives you a deeper overview, so you can see exactly which apps used the data. Why is this important? For most, it probably won't be. I'll give an example of when it helped me: I work on the go a lot; I use the wireless on my phone to connect my laptop (which is called tethering); my MacBook was set to back-up to the cloud, and little did I know it was doing this while connecting to my phone...20GB later, I was able to pinpoint what happened by looking at the data.

Below this is Hotspot & tethering. This is when you use your phone's data to connect other devices; you can use your phone's data plan, for example, to use the Internet on your iPad. Some carriers charge extra for this—mine (AT&T) includes it in the plan. To use it, tap the setting and turn it on, then name your network and password. From your other device, you find the network you set up, and connect.

Airplane mode is next. This setting turns off all wireless activity with a switch. So if your flying and they tell you to turn everything wireless of, you can do it with a switch.

Finally, Advanced is for doing some wireless connecting on a private network. This is not something a beginning user would need to do, and I'm not going to cover it, as the point of this book is to keep it ridiculously simple.

connected devices

"Connected devices" is Google's way of saying Bluetooth. If you have something that connects via Bluetooth (such as a car radio or headphones) then tap "Pair new device." If you've previously paired something, then it will show below and you can simply tap it to reconnect.

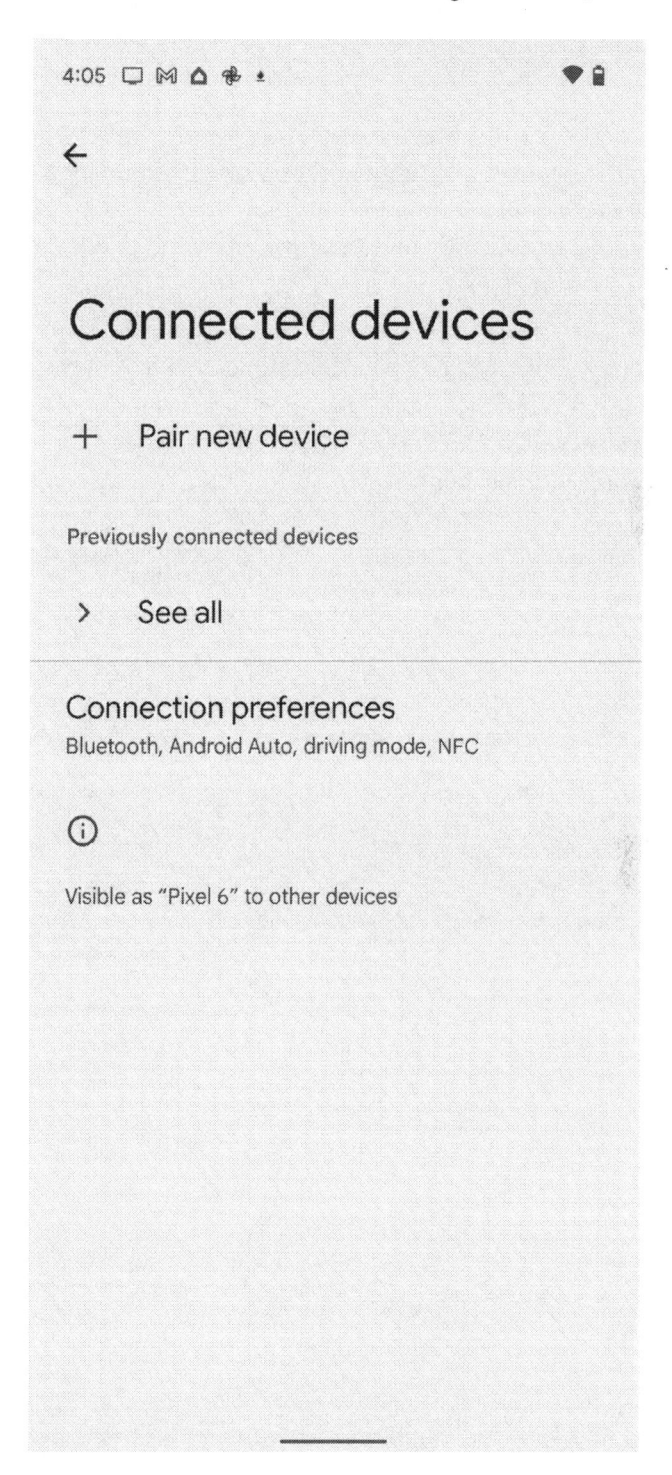

Connected devices

+ Pair new device

Previously connected devices

> See all

Connection preferences
Bluetooth, Android Auto, driving mode, NFC

ⓘ

Visible as "Pixel 6" to other devices

apps

Every app you download has different settings and permissions. A map app, for example, needs your permission to know your location. You can turn these permissions on and off here. Does it really matter? App makers can't abuse it, right? Sort of. Here's an example: a few months ago, a popular ride-sharing app made headlines because it wanted to know where passengers were after they left the ride, so they could promote different restaurants and stores and make even more money. Many felt this was both greedy and an invasion of privacy; if you are of the latter stance, then you could go in here and stop sharing your location.

4:05

←

Apps

Recently opened apps

Gmail
0 min. ago

Photos
40 min. ago

Camera
59 min. ago

> See all 59 apps

General

Default apps
Chrome, Phone, and Messages

Game settings
Turn on Game Dashboard shortcut, etc

Assistant
Hey Google and other Assistant settings

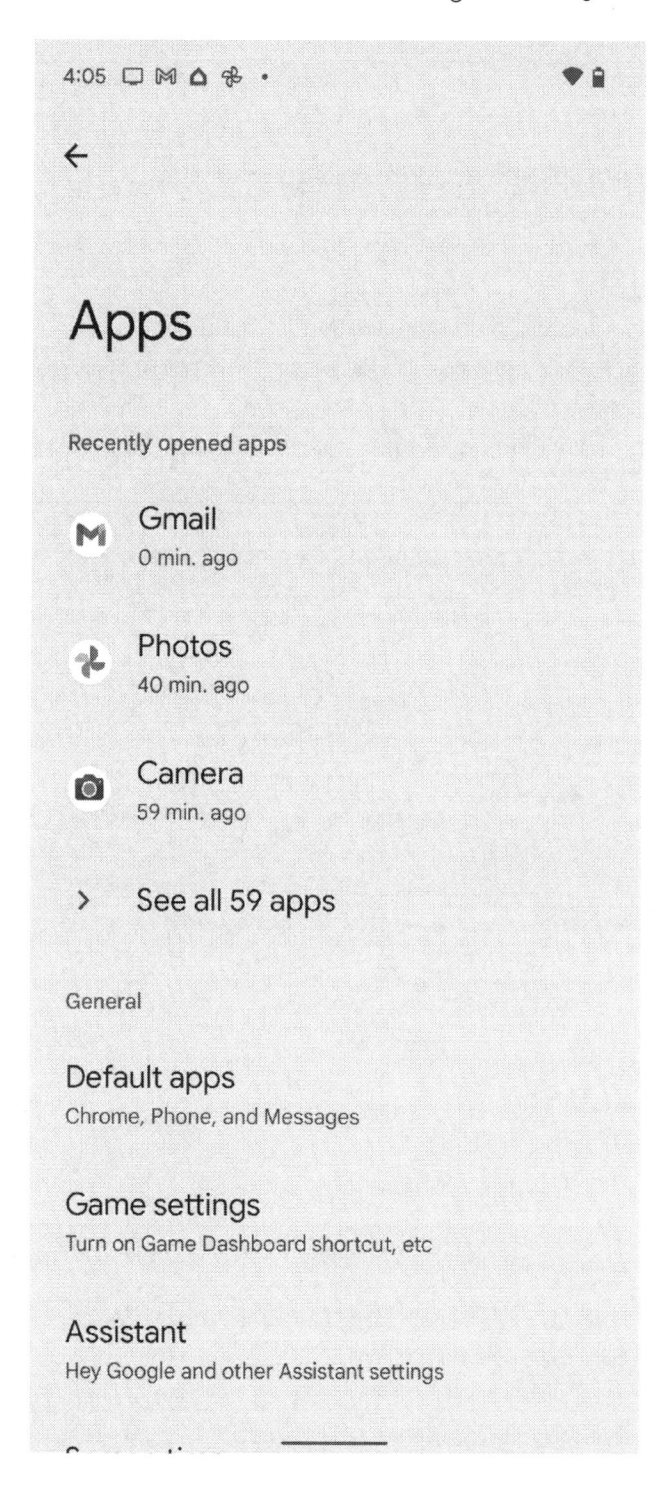

. . .

You can also use this setting to turn on Game Shortcuts.

notifications

Want to see the notifications you accidently dismissed? You can find that in the Notifications settings. You can also decide the priority people get when you get notifications. Bubbles let's conversations come in like floating icons; you can turn that on and off here.

Notifications

Manage

App settings
Control notifications from individual apps

Notification history
Show recent and snoozed notifications

Conversation

Conversations
No priority conversations

Bubbles
On / Conversations can appear as floating icons

Privacy

Device & app notifications
Control which apps and devices can read notifications

Notifications on lock screen
Show conversations, default, and silent

battery

The battery setting is more about analytics than settings you can change. There are some settings here you can edit—you can put your phone in battery saving mode, for example. This setting is more useful if your battery is draining too quickly; it helps you troubleshoot what's going on so you can get more life from your phone.

Battery

72 %

About 1 day, 4 hr left

Battery Usage
View usage for past 24 hours

Battery Saver
Off

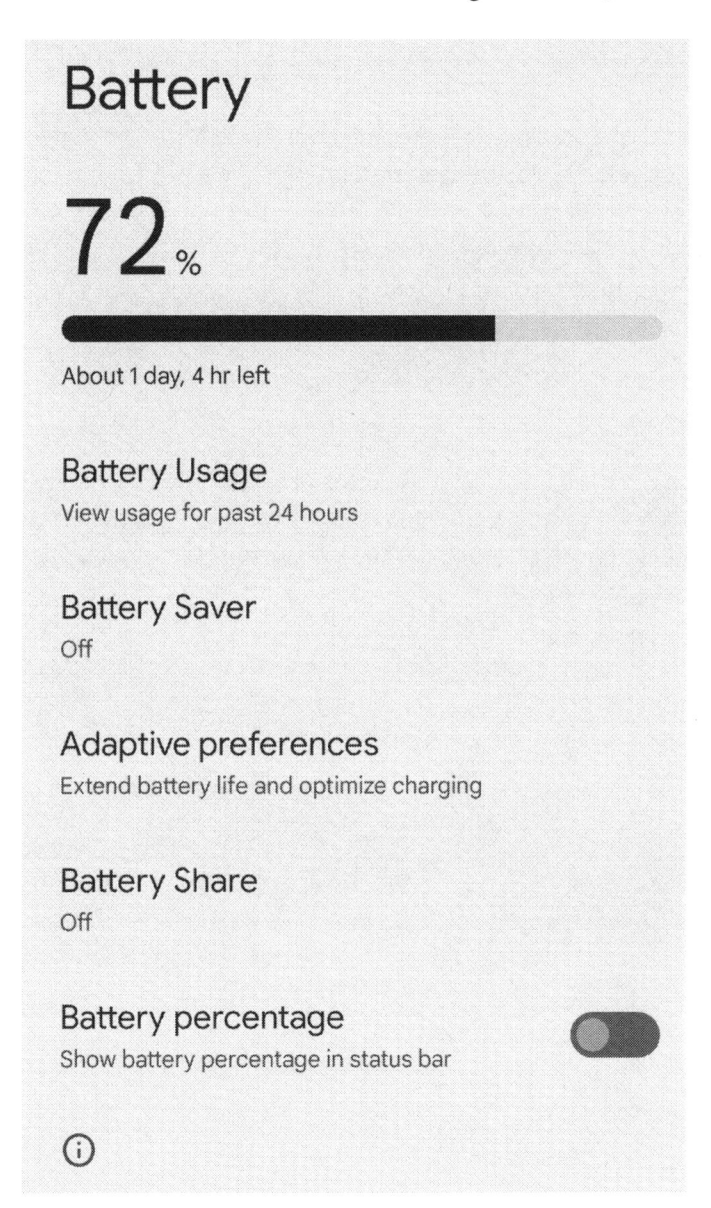

Adaptive preferences
Extend battery life and optimize charging

Battery Share
Off

Battery percentage
Show battery percentage in status bar

A Smarter Battery

Google's AI can extend into your battery life. By default, the Pixel automatically will go into Battery Saver mode when you get to 10% battery remaining. That's great. But you can also set it to go on based on your routine. So Google's AI predicts your daily habits and adjust the battery accordingly.

To use this mode, go to the System Settings app, then tap Battery and Battery Saver. Next tap Set a Schedule. Tap the option that says "Based on your routine."

storage

The Pixel has no expandable storage for SD; that means whatever you buy for your phone, that's the amount you have. You can't upgrade it later.

When you first get your phone, storage won't be a big issue, but once you start taking photos (which are larger than you think) and installing apps, it's going to go very quickly.

Storage

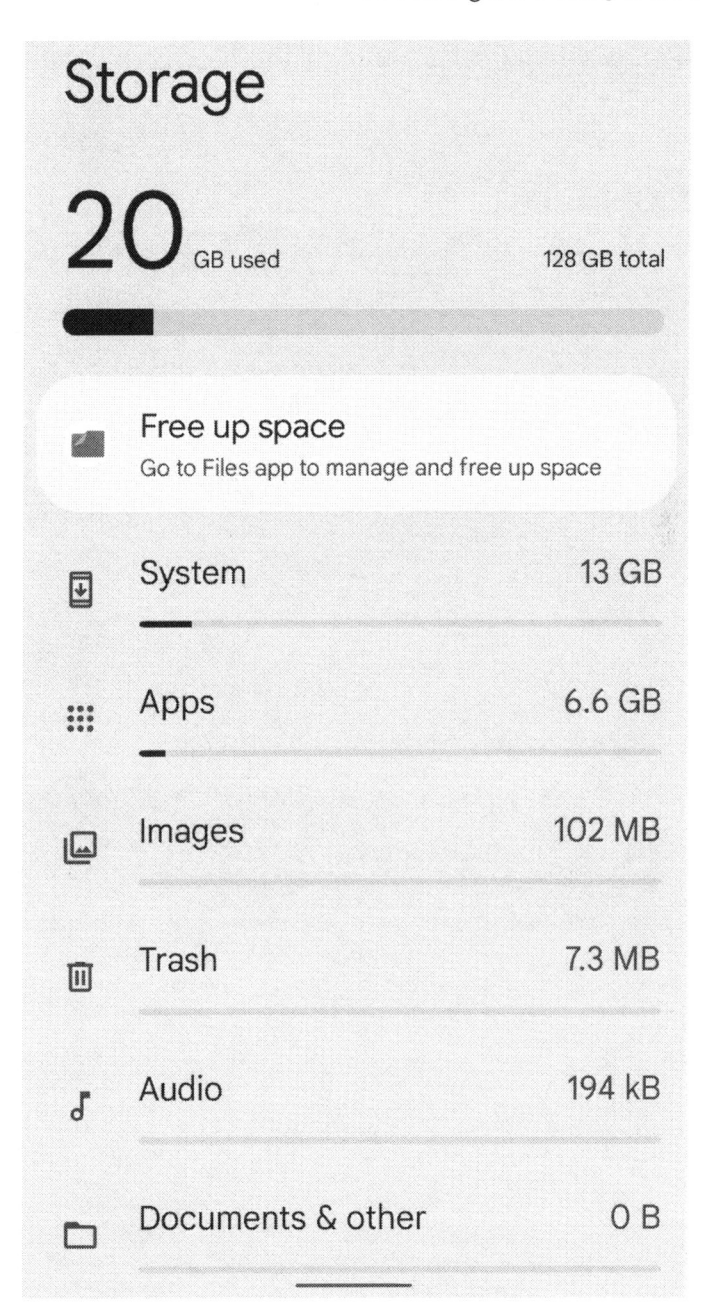

20 GB used   128 GB total

Free up space
Go to Files app to manage and free up space

System		13 GB
Apps		6.6 GB
Images		102 MB
Trash		7.3 MB
Audio		194 kB
Documents & other		0 B

The storage setting helps you manage this. It shows you what's taking up storage, so you can decide if you want to delete things. Just tap on any of the subsections and follow the instructions for what to do to save space.

sound & vibration

There's a volume button on the side of your phone, so why would you need to open up a setting for it?! This setting lets you get more specific about your volume.

For example, you may want your alarm to ring super loud in the morning, but you want your music to play very low.

Sound & vibration

♪ **Media volume**

📞 **Call volume**

🔔 **Ring & notification volume**

⏰ **Alarm volume**

Do Not Disturb
Off / 1 schedule can turn on automatically

Phone ringtone
Your New Adventure

Live Caption
Automatically caption speech

Adaptive Sound
Off

display

As with most of the settings, almost all the main features of the Display setting can be changed outside of the app. If you tap "Advanced," however, you'll see some settings not in other places. These include changing colors and font sizes.

Display

Brightness

Brightness level
41%

Adaptive brightness

Lock display

Lock screen
Show all notification content

Screen timeout
After 30 seconds of inactivity

Appearance

Dark theme
Will never turn on automatically

Font size
Default

Display size
Default

wallpaper & style

This setting is nothing more than the setting that comes when you access wallpaper from your homescreen.

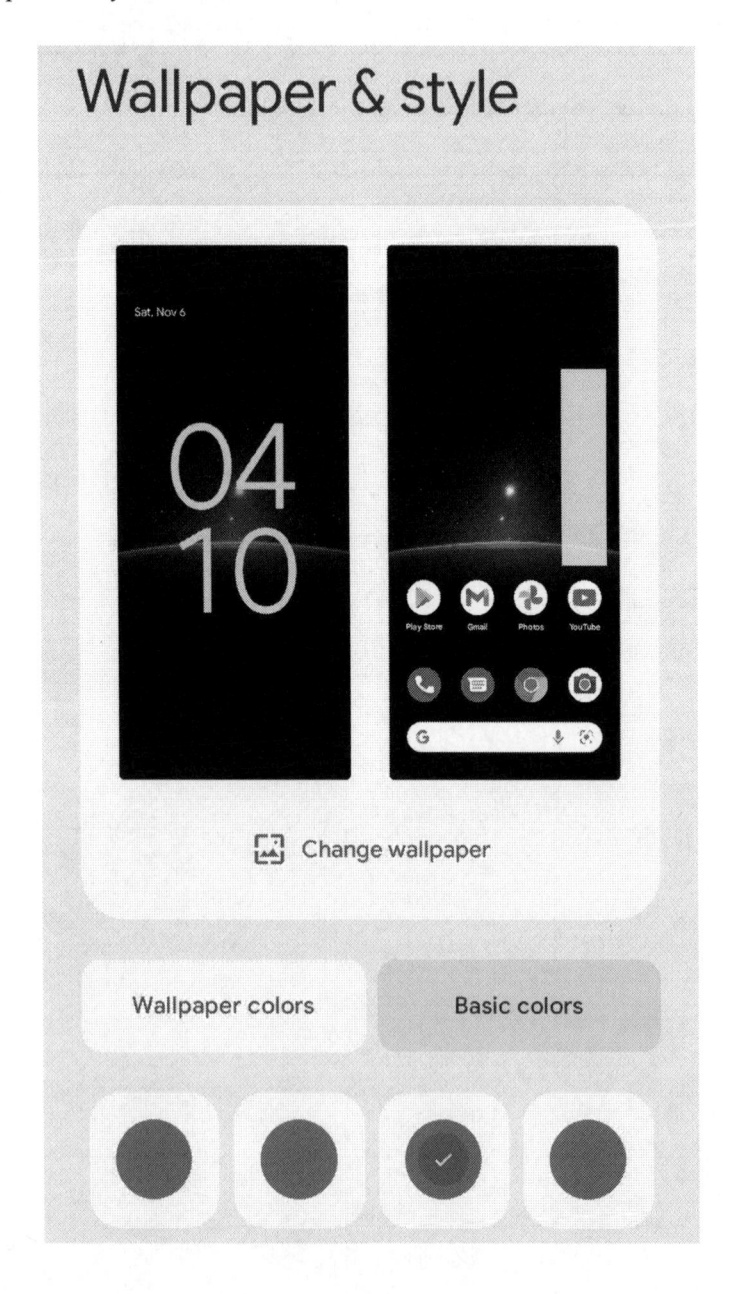

accessibility

Do you hate phones because the text is too small, the colors are all wrong, you can't hear anything? Or something else? That's where accessibility can help. This is where you make changes to the device to make it easier on your eyes or ears.

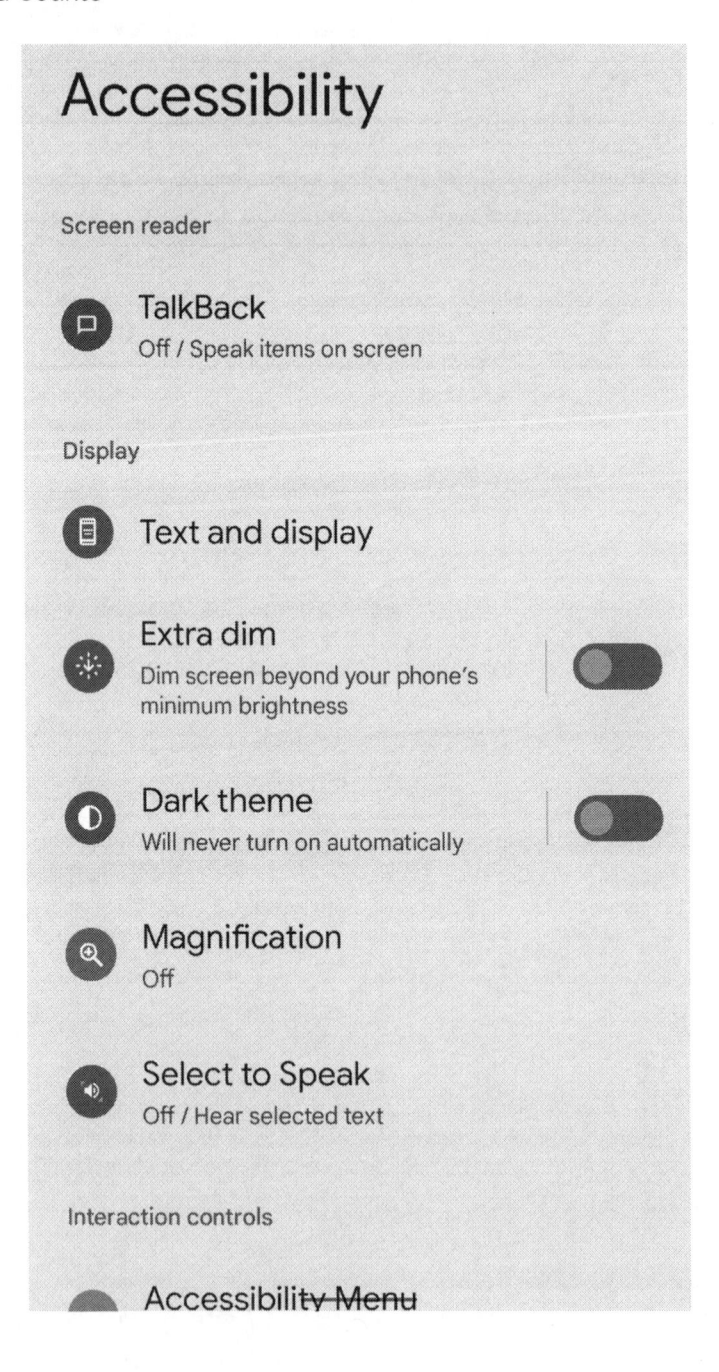

Accessibility

Screen reader

- TalkBack
  Off / Speak items on screen

Display

- Text and display

- Extra dim
  Dim screen beyond your phone's minimum brightness

- Dark theme
  Will never turn on automatically

- Magnification
  Off

- Select to Speak
  Off / Hear selected text

Interaction controls

- Accessibility ~~Menu~~

privacy

Like Location Control (covered below), Privacy settings got a big upgrade in Android 12. It's so big, it now fills an entire section in the settings.

Go to System > Privacy and tap "Advanced" to see all of them.

Privacy

Privacy dashboard
Show which apps recently used permissions

Permission manager
Control app access to your data

Camera access
For all apps and services

Microphone access
For all apps and services

Show passwords
Display characters briefly as you type

Notifications on lock screen
Show all notification content

Android System Intelligence
Get suggestions based on the people, apps, and content you interact with

Personalize using app data
Allow apps to send content to the Android system

The biggest upgrade is the ability to customize what apps see what; it's no longer all or nothing. You can refine exactly how much or how little each app can see.

The Privacy Dashboard is one of the easiest ways to see what apps are doing. In the example below, it shows in the past 24 hours, most my apps were using my location.

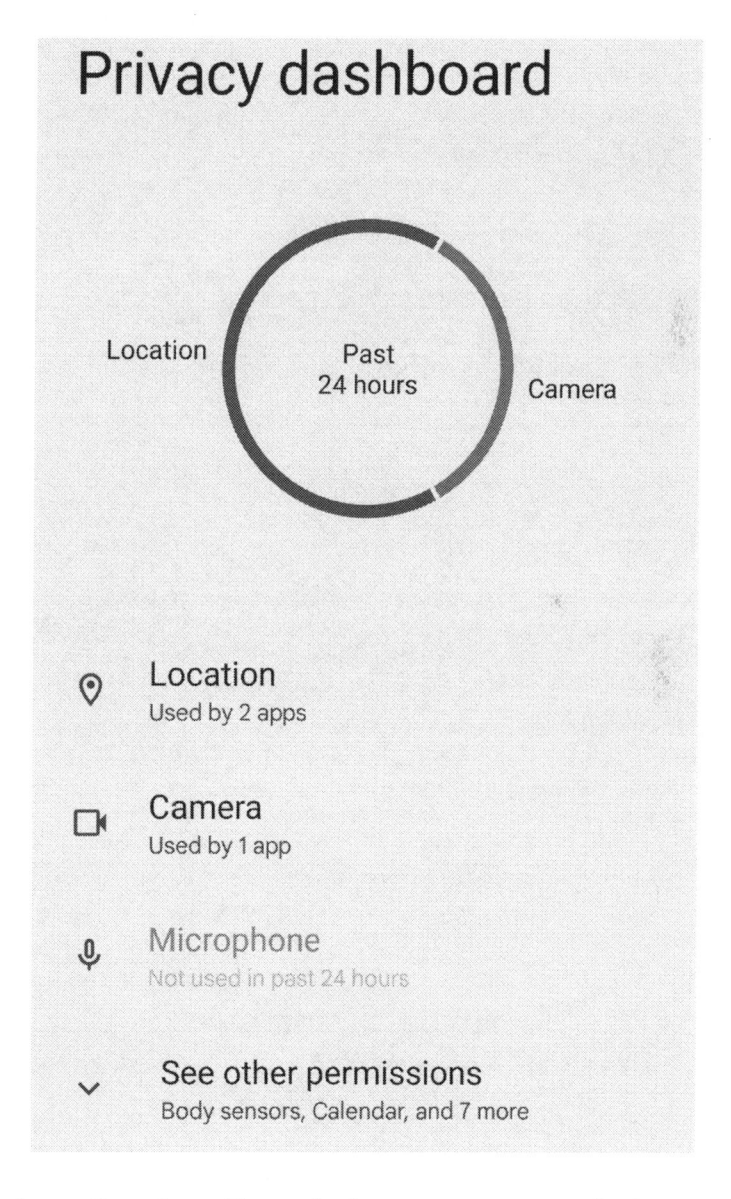

Privacy dashboard

Location — Past 24 hours — Camera

Location
Used by 2 apps

Camera
Used by 1 app

Microphone
Not used in past 24 hours

See other permissions
Body sensors, Calendar, and 7 more

Tapping on Location will reveal what apps were using the location.

Location usage

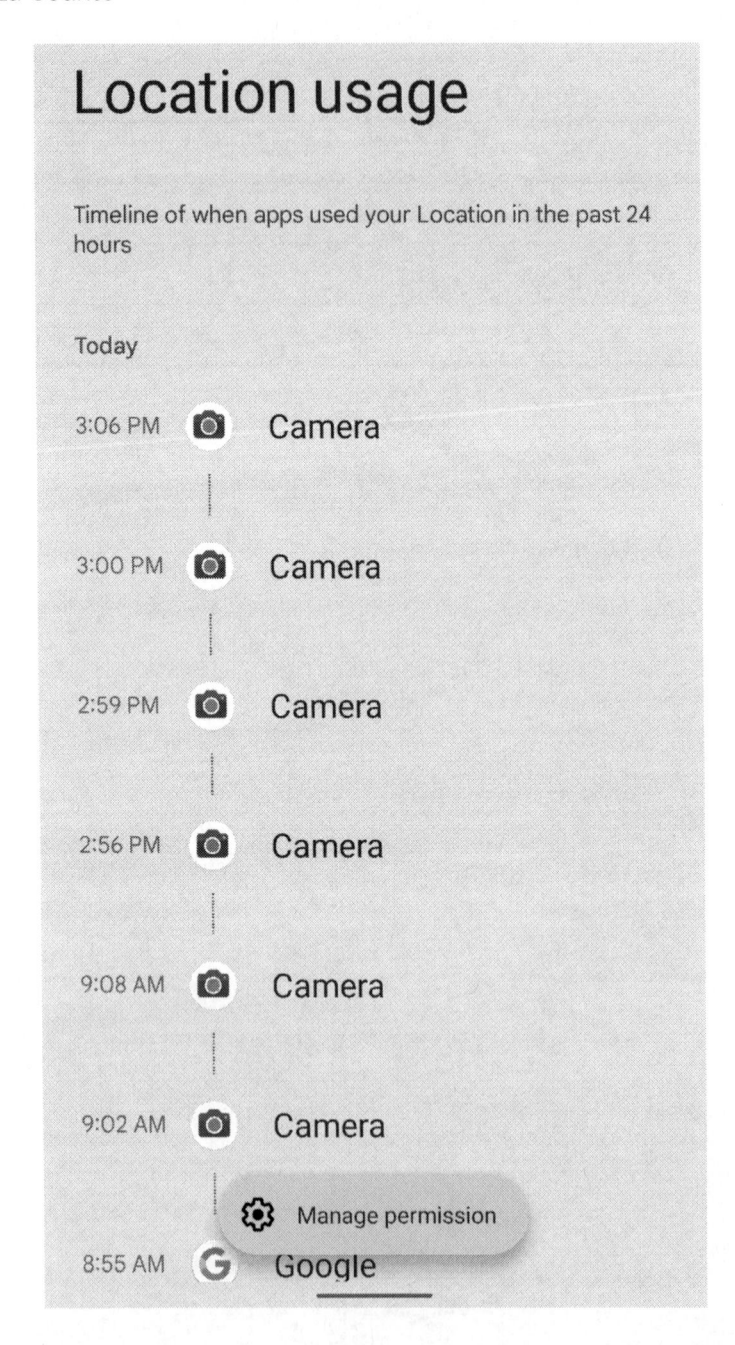

Timeline of when apps used your Location in the past 24 hours

Today

3:06 PM 📷 Camera

3:00 PM 📷 Camera

2:59 PM 📷 Camera

2:56 PM 📷 Camera

9:08 AM 📷 Camera

9:02 AM 📷 Camera

⚙️ Manage permission

8:55 AM G Google

You can then tap on Manage permissions (either on this screen or the main settings screen) to disable location sharing.

Location permission

Camera

LOCATION ACCESS FOR THIS APP

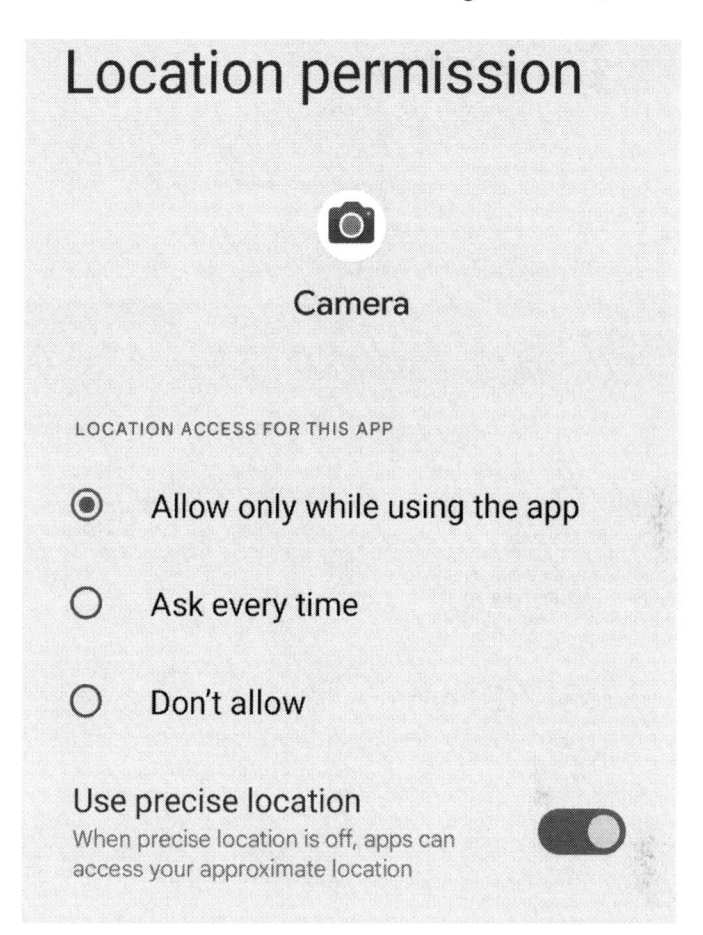

◉ Allow only while using the app

○ Ask every time

○ Don't allow

Use precise location
When precise location is off, apps can access your approximate location

security

If you want to change your lock screen, add an additional fingerprint, or turn on / off the find your phone setting, you can do it here.

Security

Security may be at risk
1 warning

⚠ You have security recommendations ✕
roboscott@gmail.com
Secure your account in the Security Checkup

Protect your account

✓ **App security**
Play Protect scanned at 8:54 AM

✓ **Find My Device**
On

✓ **Security update**
Update from November 5, 2021

location

In the past, Location Control was an all or nothing feature—you'd decide if an app could see you all the time or none of the time. That's nice for privacy, but not nice for when you actually need someone to know your location—like when you are getting picked up by a ride app like Lyft. The new Android OS adds a new option for while you are using the app. So, for example, a ride app can only see your location while you are using the app; once the ride is over, they can no longer see what you are doing.

To pick what location an app can see, go to System > Location and select the app, then tap when they can see your location.

Location

Use location

Recent access

- Camera
  65 min. ago

- Google
  7 hr. ago

> See all

App location permissions
4 of 20 apps have access to location

Location services

ⓘ

Location may use sources like GPS, Wi-Fi, mobile networks, and sensors to help estimate your device's location. Google may collect location data periodically and use this data in an anonymous way to improve location accuracy and location-based services.

safety & emergency

These settings let you add important details about you—like your blood type; they also let you enable safety features—like crash detection if your mobile device detects a motion that is common with car accidents.

Safety & emergency

Open Personal Safety

Medical information
Name, blood type and more

Emergency contacts
No information

Emergency SOS
Managed by Personal Safety

Car crash detection
Sign in to use car crash detection

Crisis alerts
Sign in to use crisis alerts

Emergency Location Service
On

Earthquake alerts
On

Wireless emergency alerts

car crash detection

Nobody hopes to use this feature, but you'll be thankful for it if the unthinkable happens. With crash detection turned on, your phone will alert emergency services if it detects you have been in a car accident. It won't call immediately, it will give you a prompt to tell you what it's doing, so if it's a mistake, you can stop it. To turn it on, go to Settings > Safety & emergency > Car crash detection.

Scott La Counte

digital wellbeing

Digital Wellbeing is my least favorite feature on the Pixel phone; now when my wife says "You spend too much time on your phone"—she can actually prove it!

The purpose of the setting is to help you manage your time more. It lets you know your spending 12 hours a day updating your social media with memes of cats, and "hopefully" make you feel like perhaps you shouldn't do that.

> # Digital Wellbeing & parental controls
>
> **Your Digital Wellbeing tools**
> Use app timers and other tools to keep track of screen time and unplug more easily
>
> Show your data
>
> **Parental controls**
> Add content restrictions and set other limits to help your child balance their screen time

google

Google is where you will go to manage any Google device connected with your phone. If you are using a Google watch, for example; or a Chromecast.

system

System is important for one very important reason: system updates. If you don't have your phone set to download updates automatically, then you'll have to do it manually here.

Tap the "Advanced" button.

This gives you a menu with more features. One is the "System update." If there's an update available, it will say it. If it says it, then tap it.

System update
Update available

You'll have to restart your phone before it downloads.

Security update available

This update fixes critical bugs and improves the performance and stability of your Pixel 3. If you download updates over the cellular network or while roaming, additional charges may apply.

Update size: 108.5 MB

Restart now

You can also change the language in this setting as well as make changes to gestures and put limits on users.

about phone

This is where you will find general information about your phone. Such as the OS you are running, the kind of phone you have, IP address, etc. It's more of an FYI, but there are a few settings here that you can change.

tips & support

This isn't really a setting. It's just tips and support. You can also talk with support here.

Help

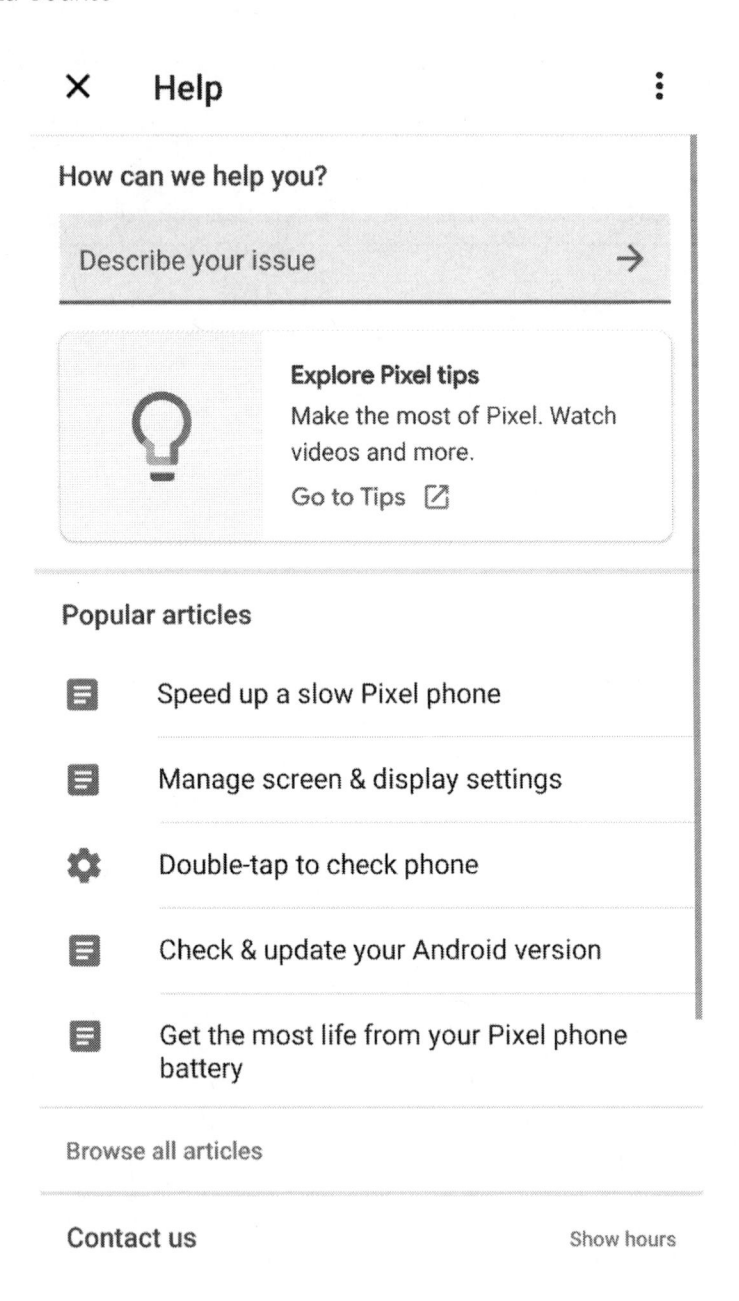

How can we help you?

Describe your issue →

Explore Pixel tips
Make the most of Pixel. Watch videos and more.
Go to Tips

Popular articles

- Speed up a slow Pixel phone
- Manage screen & display settings
- Double-tap to check phone
- Check & update your Android version
- Get the most life from your Pixel phone battery

Browse all articles

Contact us   Show hours

8 / conclusion

CONGRATULATIONS ON REACHING the end of this comprehensive guide! Together, we've explored everything from the essentials of navigating your Google Pixel 9 to unlocking its most advanced features.

As technology continues to evolve at a rapid pace, new updates will inevitably bring changes and enhancements to your Pixel 9. Staying curious and keeping up with these updates will ensure you make the most of your device's growing capabilities.

The true key to mastering your Pixel 9 lies in practice and exploration. The more you dive into its features, tweak settings, and experiment with new apps, the more you'll uncover the incredible potential of your device. Don't hesitate to explore beyond the basics—your Pixel 9 is designed to adapt to your unique needs and can achieve more than you might initially expect.

I hope this book has provided you with the tools and confidence to fully harness the power of your Google Pixel 9. Here's to countless hours of productive, enjoyable, and transformative experiences with your new device. Embrace the journey ahead and enjoy every moment!

Made in the USA
Columbia, SC
21 September 2024